First World War
and Army of Occupation
War Diary
France, Belgium and Germany

14 DIVISION
Divisional Troops
Divisional Ammunition Column
10 May 1915 - 18 June 1919

WO95/1888/2

The Naval & Military Press Ltd
www.nmarchive.com
Published in association with The National Archives

Published by

The Naval & Military Press Ltd

Unit 10 Ridgewood Industrial Park,

Uckfield, East Sussex,

TN22 5QE England

Tel: +44 (0) 1825 749494

www.naval-military-press.com

www.nmarchive.com

This diary has been reprinted in facsimile from the original. Any imperfections are inevitably reproduced and the quality may fall short of modern type and cartographic standards.

© **Crown Copyright**
Images reproduced by permission of The National Archives, London, England, 2015.

Contents

Document type	Place/Title	Date From	Date To
Heading	1888/2 14th Divisional Ammunition Column		
Heading	14th Division 14th Divl Ammn Column May 1915-Jun 1919		
Miscellaneous	14th D A C Vol 7		
Heading	14th Division 48th Brigade R.F.A. (ammunition Column) Vol I 11-5-30-6.15		
War Diary		30/06/1915	30/06/1915
Heading	14th Divisional Ammunition Column Vol:I 10-5-5-8-15		
War Diary	Aldershot	10/05/1915	23/05/1915
War Diary	Havre	23/05/1915	28/05/1915
War Diary	Borre	29/05/1915	31/05/1915
War Diary	Westoutre	01/06/1915	05/08/1915
Heading	14th Division 14th D.A.C. Vol 2 August To Oct 15		
War Diary	Watou	07/08/1915	21/10/1915
Heading	14th Division Nov 15		
War Diary	Watou (L1a Map Sheet 27)	01/11/1915	29/11/1915
Heading	14th D.A.C. Vol:4		
War Diary	Watou	05/12/1915	30/12/1915
Miscellaneous	Return	21/12/1915	21/12/1915
Miscellaneous	Return	20/12/1915	20/12/1915
Miscellaneous	Nominal Roll Head Quarters 14th Bint Ammn. Column		
Miscellaneous	Nominal Roll Of No 1 Section 14 DAG Column RFA	19/12/1915	19/12/1915
Miscellaneous			
Miscellaneous	Nominal Roll Of No I Section-14th D.A.C.	19/12/1915	19/12/1915
Miscellaneous			
Miscellaneous	Nominal Roll 3rd Section 14th D.A.B.		
Miscellaneous	14th D.A.C Vol.5 Jan 16		
War Diary	Watou	04/01/1916	30/01/1916
Heading	14th D.A.C. Vol. 6		
War Diary	St. Sixte	01/02/1916	22/02/1916
War Diary	Lignereuil	22/02/1916	22/02/1916
War Diary	Beauval	25/02/1916	25/02/1916
War Diary	St. Vaste	23/02/1916	28/02/1916
War Diary	Lingeruil	01/03/1916	06/03/1916
War Diary	Barly	06/03/1916	19/03/1916
War Diary	Hauteville	19/03/1916	30/06/1916
War Diary	Berneville	30/06/1916	30/06/1916
Heading	War Diary Of 14th Divisional Ammunition Column From 1st July 1916 To 31st July 1916 (Volume 15)		
War Diary	Berneville	01/07/1916	05/07/1916
War Diary	Hauteville	05/07/1916	29/07/1916
Heading	War Diary Of 14th Divisional Ammunition Column From 1st August To 31st August. (Volume XVI)		
Miscellaneous	Staff capt R.A. 14th Div	02/09/1916	02/09/1916
War Diary	Hauteville	04/08/1916	10/08/1916
War Diary	Meaulte	11/08/1916	31/08/1916
Heading	War Diary Of 14th Divisional Amm. Col. For. September 1916. Volume XVII.		
War Diary	Meaulte	01/09/1916	17/09/1916
War Diary	Montauban	17/09/1916	30/09/1916

Heading	War Diary Of 14th Divisional Ammunition Column. From October 1st To October 31st 1916 Volume XVIII		
War Diary	Montauban	01/10/1916	31/10/1916
Heading	War Diary Of 14th Divisional Ammunition Column From 1st November 1916 To 30th November 1916 (Volume)		
War Diary	Fosseux	01/11/1916	21/11/1916
Heading	War Diary Of 14th Divisional Ammunition Column From 1st December 1916. To, 31st December 1916. (Volume)		
War Diary	Fosseux	02/12/1916	23/12/1916
War Diary	War Diary Of 14th Divisional Ammunition Column. From-January 1st. 1917. To-January 31st. 1917		
War Diary	Ivergny	02/01/1917	08/01/1917
War Diary	Gouy	08/01/1917	31/01/1917
Heading	War Diary Of 14th Divisional Ammunition Column. From 1st February, 1917 To 28th February, 1917 Volume 22.		
War Diary	Barly	03/02/1917	27/02/1917
Heading	War Diary Of 14th Divisional Ammunition Column. From 1st March. 1917 To-31st March, 1917 Volume 23		
War Diary	Barly	10/03/1917	21/03/1917
War Diary	Simencourt	23/03/1917	31/03/1917
Heading	War Diary For D.A.C. (14th) 1st April To 30th 1917 Volume 24		
War Diary	Simencourt.	04/04/1917	30/04/1917
Heading	War Diary Of 14th Divisional Ammunition Column. Volume 25.		
War Diary	Simencourt.	01/05/1917	17/05/1917
War Diary	Agny	17/05/1917	27/06/1917
War Diary	Etree-Wamin	28/06/1917	28/06/1917
War Diary	Croix	29/06/1917	30/06/1917
Heading	War Diary Of 14th Divisional Ammunition Column. From-July 1st, 1917 To July-31st, 1917 Volume 27.		
War Diary	Nedonchelle	01/07/1917	01/07/1917
War Diary	Neuf Pre	02/07/1917	02/07/1917
War Diary	Rouge-Croix	03/07/1917	03/07/1917
War Diary	Bailleul	04/07/1917	05/07/1917
War Diary	Dranoutre	05/07/1917	11/07/1917
War Diary	Bailleul	11/07/1917	30/07/1917
Heading	War Diary For 14th Divisional Ammunition Column For August-1917 Volume 28		
War Diary	Bailleul	04/08/1917	10/08/1917
War Diary	Ouderdom	11/08/1917	31/08/1917
Heading	War Diary For 14th Divisional Ammunition Column RFA For September 1917. Vol 25		
War Diary	Ouderdom	01/09/1917	05/09/1917
War Diary	Neuve Eglise	06/09/1917	30/09/1917
Heading	War Diary For October-1917 Of 14th Divisional Ammunition Column R.F.A. Volume 30		
War Diary	Neuve Eglise	03/10/1917	31/10/1917
Heading	War Diary For November 1917 14th. Divisional Ammunition Column R.F.A. Volume XXXI.		
War Diary	Neuve Eglise	02/11/1917	11/11/1917
War Diary	Watou	18/11/1917	20/11/1917
War Diary	Vlamertinghe	24/11/1917	30/11/1917

Heading	War Diaries For December 1917 14th D.A.G. & vol 28		
War Diary	Vlamertinghe	03/12/1917	01/01/1918
War Diary	Oudezeele	02/01/1918	02/01/1918
War Diary	Renescure	03/01/1918	05/01/1918
War Diary	Etinehem	06/01/1918	23/01/1918
War Diary	Sept Fours	24/01/1918	24/01/1918
War Diary	Guiscard	25/01/1918	26/01/1918
War Diary	Cugny	30/01/1918	03/02/1918
War Diary	Detroit Bleu	05/02/1918	28/02/1918
Heading	14th Divisional Artillery 14th Divisional Ammunition Column R.F.A. March 1918		
War Diary	Detroit Bleu.	01/03/1918	19/03/1918
War Diary	Guivry Beaugies	21/03/1918	21/03/1918
War Diary	Beaugies	22/03/1918	22/03/1918
War Diary	Grissoles	22/03/1918	22/03/1918
War Diary	Beaurains	23/03/1918	23/03/1918
War Diary	Plessis Chcheleux	24/03/1918	24/03/1918
War Diary	Lassigny	25/03/1918	25/03/1918
War Diary	Marest Sur Matz.	26/03/1918	28/03/1918
War Diary	Arsy	29/03/1918	29/03/1918
War Diary	Noroy	30/03/1918	30/03/1918
War Diary	Abbeville St. Lucien	31/03/1918	31/03/1918
Heading	War Diary 14th Divisional Ammunition Column. April 1918		
War Diary	Saulchoy	01/04/1918	01/04/1918
War Diary	Contre	02/04/1918	04/04/1918
War Diary	Vers.	05/04/1918	05/04/1918
War Diary	Blangy Tronville	06/04/1918	06/04/1918
War Diary	Glisy	06/04/1918	17/04/1918
War Diary	Ailly Sur Somme	18/04/1918	20/04/1918
War Diary	Westrehen	21/04/1918	28/04/1918
War Diary	Lapugnoy	29/04/1918	31/05/1918
Heading	War Diary Of 14th Divisional Ammunition Column, R.F.A. From 1/6/18 To 30/6/18 Volume 38		
War Diary	Lapugnoy	01/06/1918	31/07/1918
Miscellaneous	Ref A S 129/8		
War Diary	Southampton	01/07/1918	01/07/1918
War Diary	Havre	02/07/1918	03/07/1918
War Diary	Jealingthan	04/07/1918	04/07/1918
War Diary	Hardinghem	04/07/1918	10/07/1918
War Diary	Clerques.	10/07/1918	11/07/1918
War Diary	Fournehem	11/07/1918	12/07/1918
War Diary	Blue Ellaission	12/07/1918	22/07/1918
War Diary	Fournehem	22/07/1918	30/07/1918
War Diary	Lapugnoy	04/08/1918	31/08/1918
Miscellaneous	A A Q M G 14 Div		
War Diary	Fournehem	01/08/1918	14/08/1918
War Diary	Lumbres	14/08/1918	16/08/1918
War Diary	Fournehem	16/08/1918	22/08/1918
War Diary	Lederzeele	23/08/1918	23/08/1918
War Diary	Wormhoudt	24/08/1918	24/08/1918
War Diary	Harrow Camp	25/08/1918	29/08/1918
War Diary	28/A 25 b-0-8	31/08/1918	31/08/1918
War Diary	Lapugnoy	01/09/1918	02/09/1918
War Diary	Choques	11/09/1918	16/09/1918
War Diary	Steenbecque	17/09/1918	18/09/1918

War Diary	Steenvoorde	19/09/1918	26/09/1918
War Diary	Reninghelst	28/09/1918	01/10/1918
War Diary	Neuve Eglise	02/10/1918	17/10/1918
War Diary	Gapaard	17/10/1918	17/10/1918
War Diary	Korentje	18/10/1918	18/10/1918
War Diary	La Vignette	19/10/1918	20/10/1918
War Diary	Tourcoing	21/10/1918	04/11/1918
War Diary	37/A 24 B 9.1.	04/11/1918	06/12/1918
War Diary	37/A 21c 95 70	08/12/1918	30/01/1919
War Diary	In The Field	01/02/1919	19/02/1919
War Diary	Watterlos France	21/02/1919	28/02/1919
War Diary	Estaimbourg Belgium	01/04/1919	28/04/1919
War Diary	Estaimbourg	30/04/1919	18/06/1919

1888/2
14th Divisional Ammunition
Column

14TH DIVISION

14TH DIVL AMMN COLUMN
MAY 1915 - JUN 1919

14ᵗʰ D A C
Vol # 7

b/6711

a2/a96

14th Division

48th Brigade R.F.A.
(Ammunition Column.)

Vol. I.

11-5-30-6-15

Army Form C. 2118.

WAR DIARY
or
INTELLIGENCE SUMMARY.
(Erase heading not required.)

48th Bde. Amm. Col. R.F.A.

Place	Date	Hour	Summary of Events and Information	Remarks and references to Appendices
	30/6/15		Tuesday. May 11th. Received orders to mobilize	
			May 12-20 Nothing special to report.	
			Friday. May 21 Entrained at Southampton	
			Saturday " 22 Nothing special to report	
			Sunday " 23 Disembarked at Havre	
			Monday " 24 Entrained	
			Tuesday " 25 Detained at St. Omer. Marched to Ledergele	
			Wednesday " 26 Nothing special to report	
			Thursday " 27 Marched up & marched to Brelle.	
			Friday " 28 Left Brielle. Marched to Moulinacre	
			Saturday " 29 Nothing special to report	
			Sunday " 30 Left Moulinacre for Lavender	
			Monday " 31	
			Tuesday. June 1st ⎫	
			Wednesday " 2 ⎬ Nothing special to report	
			Thursday " 3 ⎪	
			Friday " 4 ⎭	
			Saturday " 5 2/Lieut. W.R. Cowie joined unit to replace Lieut.	
			Sunday " 6 moved posted to "B" Battery 48th Bde.	
			Monday " 7 Nothing special to report	
			Tuesday " 8 ⎫	
			Wednesday " 9 ⎬	
			Thursday " 10 ⎪ Nothing special to report	
			Friday " 11 ⎪	
			Saturday " 12 ⎪	
			Sunday " 13 ⎭	

WAR DIARY
or
INTELLIGENCE SUMMARY.
(Erase heading not required.)

Army Form C. 2118.

Place	Date	Hour	Summary of Events and Information	Remarks and references to Appendices
	Monday June 14		Nothing special to report	
	Tuesday " 15		2 Lieut J.S. Watson joined unit vice 2 Lieut W.R. Eerie	
	Wednesday " 16		Moved to O'Reilly 10½ ???	
	Thursday " 17		Nothing special to report	
	Friday " 18		"	
	Saturday " 19		Moved column to rendezvous to meet Brigade. Marched to point 1½ miles N.W. of Watou & took up billets in that area.	
	Sunday " 20		Nothing special to report	
	Monday " 21st		Moved column to point S.E. of Watou & took up fresh billets	
	Tuesday " 22			
	Wednesday " 23			
	Thursday " 24 ⎫		Nothing special to report	
	Friday " 25 ⎬			
	Saturday " 26 ⎭			
	Sunday " 27			
	Monday " 28		Moved to advance billeting area. Took up billets	
	Tuesday " 29 ⎫		Nothing special to report.	
	Wednesday " 30 ⎭			

E. Wall .... CAPT. R.F.A.
COMDG. AMMUNITION COLUMN, R.F.A.

14th. Kurram.

14 to Divisional Ammunition Column

Vol: I

WD 10-5-5- 5-15

June '19

127/6250

Army Form C. 2118.

14 D.A.C. — R.F.A

WAR DIARY
~~INTELLIGENCE SUMMARY~~
(Erase heading not required.)

Instructions regarding War Diaries and Intelligence Summaries are contained in F. S. Regs., Part II. and the Staff Manual respectively. Title pages will be prepared in manuscript.

Place	Date	Hour	Summary of Events and Information	Remarks and references to Appendices
Aldershot	10-5-15	m/n/n	14 D.A.C.	
	11-5-15		Orders Khatby. 1st Section 1-2&3 draw stores - Ammunition - Pack Ammunition waggons - Parade of all ranks - checks equipment & clothing - Pay books identity disks issued. - Horse Mules examined by Vet Off. - Shoeing continues.	
	12-5-15		Continue drawing Skin, ammunition, harness renewals - stout clean accounts.	
	13—		Parade - pack waggons - General fatigues - storing completes - harness roll & documents completed ready of dispatch.	
	14		Continue packing waggons - drawing returning store equipment - completing clothing equipment - ordnance harness waggon.	
	15		Drill order for all ranks - O.C. inspection - checking clothing & returning surplus. Kits filed destroyed. - Drawing ammunition.	
	16		Drawing Ammunition. Dust inspection by M.O. Church Parade. Waggon inspection.	
	17		G.S. packing new - checking contents waggons - Rifle inspection.	
	18		Re-packing waggons - drawing new stat. equipment - Drew ambulance Horses & 1 waggon & Service waggon - Service Jobpin - Service Inspection - Service packing of surplus kits - Plate left behind i/c Chap 1 2nd Lt Palmer. H.L.	

1577 Wt. W10791/1773 500,000 1/15 D.D. & L. A.D.S.S./Forms/C. 2118.

Army Form C. 2118.

WAR DIARY
or
INTELLIGENCE SUMMARY.

14 B/C R.F.A

(Erase heading not required.)

Instructions regarding War Diaries and Intelligence Summaries are contained in F. S. Regs., Part II. and the Staff Manual respectively. Title pages will be prepared in manuscript.

Place	Date	Hour	Summary of Events and Information	Remarks and references to Appendices
Aldershot	19.5.15		Divl Service heading nos - Divl Inspection by O.C. Ranks'horses for see ranks fully equipped - Inspecting Quarters when vacated.	
"	20.		D.S. heading no Inspection by O.C. Column — Quarters Cleaned & Inspn Spent own Clothing burnt	
	21		Begun inputs - vouchers not attes. Com is from Divl Stores to Randl Chec. Section 1.2 & 3 entrain as for being Advanced for Embarking at Sow. SOUTHAMPTON	
	22		Arrival at SOUTHAMPTON of 1st Train & others Continue training at 1 hour Interval. As hand load/arrive train an entils) 3 Hour cart fr Catoril All aboard 4 boats at 4 P.M. Livestock nd chkd - 2 21st Sept May Train loads spection loads mgs 5 up which cause confusion plans of kit etc	
	23		Arrive at HAVRE of NP. & part of 1-3 Section on transports M Aiden "Anglo Canadian". Huge task trans'n at own lines causing congestion on Quay side — Men no other transports not arrived — Innsufficient men & both after horses wagons, wagon loaded n Quay side stowen & men proceed to	

WAR DIARY
or
INTELLIGENCE SUMMARY.
(Erase heading not required.)

Army Form C. 2118.

14 Bde. R.F.A.

Place	Date	Hour	Summary of Events and Information	Remarks and references to Appendices
Havre	23	1 p.m.	Weather very hot. Camp v. comfortable. Remainder of Column arrive in Camp. No 3 section commence to entrain 4 p.m. at HAVRE station. Difficulty experienced in getting mules in French trucks - no heart rope provided by G.1098 - Sent to the Ordnance & form - arrived just in time.	
	23/24		Entraining of the section continues	
	25		Commenced training at ST OMER at 8 p.m. Thence & billets at GANSPETTE about 9 miles away	
	26	1 am	Arrive GANSPETTE - very fine.	
		4 am	Supp. Train too arrives & entrains at intervals until 4 p.m.. 2 mules lost - my groups on y train. 1 gets free down a Quay & left in charge of T.O. at HAVRE	
	27		Rested at GANSPETTE - Several Interprete attacks. Bde may arrived.	
	28		March to BUYSSCHEURE & billet there	
	29		March early in morning to BORRE & billet there	
BORRE	29		Remain in billet	

WAR DIARY or INTELLIGENCE SUMMARY

Army Form C. 2118.

14. D.A.C. R.F.A.

Place	Date	Hour	Summary of Events and Information	Remarks and references to Appendices
BORRE	31/5/15	8.30 am	Left BORRE by Road & Rail — 1 man sent to Base Impure — Arrived in NEUVE ÉGLISE about 12 noon. In Belgium. Drew rations, road to WESTOUTRE	
WESTOUTRE		1 pm.	No 2 Section sent up to billet in farm 1 mile NE of WESTOUTRE & an advanced section	
	1/6/15		Battery Am. Col. demands. Hampenner Monts etc had under & receive any thro 14 D's Am Col	
"	2		Howitzer ammunition (8 wagons) despatched, under 2/Lt Newitt, attached to 46 D's Am. Col. to serve 3 batteries of 49 Bryans R.F.A	
"	3rd		2/Lt Covie posted to 1 A.C. brigade. 2 Lt. Forbes a casualty.	
"	11		1/2 Lt Miles-Hamon arrives from Base to replace 2/Lt Covie.	
"	13		2 Lt. Standwich on posts to B/48 in exchange of 2/Lt McHugh — 11 to No 3 Section	
"	"		1 Sergt, 1 Corp + No 3 Sherry Smith arrived as reinforcement from Base.	
"	14		2/Lt Walsh posts to Miyaw — joined next day.	
"	19		Orders to move to West of POPERINGHE tomorrow.	

Army Form C. 2118.

WAR DIARY
or
INTELLIGENCE SUMMARY.
(Erase heading not required.)

14 D.A.C. — R.F.A

Place	Date	Hour	Summary of Events and Information	Remarks and references to Appendices
WESTOUTRE	13/6/15	11.30	Route march to nr Biellt between WATOU & STEENVOORDE. H.Q. at K.21.a.55.	
	18°		No.2 Sect K21C97, No.3 Sect at K21a55. No.1 Sect K21.c.10.5.	
			2/Lt. F.T. Harris & 2/Lt A.J.L. Hornby joined from base.	
			Handed over K28 D.A.C. R.F.A. 15 N.C.Os. Men & 3 complete Waggons — these were part	
			of our Horsitzn portion & permanent parts to 28 Div.	
	26"	10.0	Route march to Biellt between WATOU & ABEELE.	
			Remainder of Horsitzn waggons were attached as a separate unit under Lt. Alexander, they were attached to 49 Brigade R.F.A. which was attached to the 3rd Division. They are exempted at G.9 & 83 Maps 28 & 49,000	
	28°	1.30p	Route march to tat camp West of POPERINGHE. L.11.C.44 sheet 27.	
	29.		2/Lt Garrett posted away to C/49	
	1st July		2/Lt K.C. Haddow & 2/Lt N.E. Boys joined from base.	
	3"	—	Major Herbert directing horse transport inspected all animals of Column & gave lecture & W.O. Stenn.	
	4"		S.C.R.A. inspected Waggon Lines of Div Artillery & reported that the units management of Horses, lines etc was Excellent.	

WAR DIARY or INTELLIGENCE SUMMARY.

Army Form C. 2118.

14 BAC RFA

Place	Date	Hour	Summary of Events and Information	Remarks and references to Appendices
	6/7/15		A party NCOs & men were detailed as instructors to Gun drill with the 48th Brigade to their rest area	
	7.		Received a draft of 1 NCO, 12 gunners & drivers from base	
	9.		2/Lt. J.J. Hawks posted to 49 B.A. Col.	
	10.		Men returned from Gun drill instruction	
	14.		2/Lt. Sn Sn Arthur Thompson posted to 14 BAC	
			Capt. R.B. Grivas to take over the column of Hq. 46 Brigade R.F.A & to take on command of No. 3 Sectn.	
	21.		Lt. T.W.E. Davis posted to 46 Brigade R.F.A. Lt. Keys also to 46 Bde.	
	23.		2/Lt. B.J. Alexander & 2/Lt. I. Senior posted to 49 Brigade	
	26.		Deurys to carry on Charge of WATOU Lia. Hosp Shed 27.	
	29.		Lt. X Slater posted for this unit & clearing hospital suffering from dysentery	
	22.		1st May from sick & clearing station onward than suffering from influenza	
	30.		Officers joined the base. 2/Lt Cann Roden 2/Lt Wardens & 2/Lt Wood	
	1 August		4/13 Cairo Gache posted to 47 Brigade R.F.A.)	
	5.		2/Lt Todd posted to 49 Brigade R.F.A	
			On the night of 30/31 July the 14 Div were in action & an ammunition case for	AHL

1577 Wt.W10791/1773 500,000 1/15 D. D. & L. A.D.S.S./Forms/C. 2118.

WAR DIARY
or
INTELLIGENCE SUMMARY.

14 BAC — RFA

Army Form C. 2118.

Place	Date	Hour	Summary of Events and Information	Remarks and references to Appendices
			Ammunition was made by this unit was actually never to not the III carts to be advance section. The ammunition was truly supplies direct to the BACs by the Park in Motor Lorries. It appears at present that horse transport for a BAC is quite unsuitable and better results were economy would be obtained from mechanical transport in at least say one section only. Perhaps 4 the other two mechanical transport. In the recent engagement the Motor Lorries of the Park supplied ammunition from Railhead to BACs direct over a distance of 30 miles — Horse transport could not possibly have supplied the quantity of ammunition in the time.	Atty

121/7594

14th Division

14th Div. A.C.
vol 2
August to Oct 15

WAR DIARY
or
INTELLIGENCE SUMMARY.
(Erase heading not required.)

Army Form C. 2118

14 D.A.C. - R.F.A

Instructions regarding War Diaries and Intelligence Summaries are contained in F.S. Regs., Part II. and the Staff Manual respectively. Title pages will be prepared in manuscript.

Place	Date	Hour	Summary of Events and Information	Remarks and references to Appendices
WATOU	7 Aug		2nd Lt Lathw. un posted to the 4 & 8 Brigade	
"	2 Aug		2 Lt Davies un posted 46 Brigade & Lt Slater seconded England	
"	4 Aug		2 Lt J.J. McKeown & F.E. Harper & H Jamain & D. Mackenzie & Bennett posted to the column. They arrived the base.	
"	15.		2 Lt J.D. Mackenzie posted to R.H.A. & 7 Brigade & 2 Lt Jamain to the 46 Brigade & 2 Lt J.J. McKeown to 4 Brigade. 2 Lt G.G. Taylor joins for the Amm. Park	
"	9.		Capt Carteyen ceases to command No II Section & leaves for England. Capt Stuart joins for 46 Brigade.	
"	10		2 Lt. R.J. Grove & Lt G. Holman joins the column for No II Section. 2 Lt H.J. Grove	
"	18		2 Lt J.E. Hay posted to 45 Brigade R.F.A.	
"	19		M. A.S.H. O'Brien 2Lt H.V. Petrie joins the column for the base. Capt Lennon	
"			1 Pro I Sect posted to 47 & 15 A.C. 1 Pro III Section was relieved of duty as Advances section by No II section	
"	20		2 Lt F.S. O'Brien arrived from 22 T.H. Battery & posted 39. F.H. Battery	
"	26.		2 Lt W.B. Bennett posted to the 48 Brigade for III section	
"	30 Sept 1		Leave started for this unit.	

Army Form C. 2118

WAR DIARY
or
INTELLIGENCE SUMMARY.   14 DAC RFA

(Erase heading not required.)

Instructions regarding War Diaries and Intelligence Summaries are contained in F. S. Regs., Part II. and the Staff Manual respectively. Title pages will be prepared in manuscript.

Place	Date	Hour	Summary of Events and Information	Remarks and references to Appendices
WATOU	Sept 7	—	Major Stenhouse R.G.A reported to relieve Capt Stewart who applies for Comdg Summary. Took over of Capt Stewart II sects 8" unit.	
	11		2/Lt S.S. Bradley & 2/Lt W.C. Taylor arrived from depôt to No I & III Sections respectively	
	13		Inspecting trenches by A.D.V.S.	
	15		2/Lt J.D. Taylor posted from this unit to 746 B.M.R.C.A. 2/Lt E.R. Moye posted to No II Sect from #6 B.ac Capt L.D. Green invalided. 2/Lt J. divisional area	
	23		Capt Stewart posted to No 1 Sect. 2/Lt Pelling posted from No 1 & III Sect.	
	4 Oct		No 1 Sect. lorries delayed. Ammunition sent from No II sect the delay being caused by the enormous amount of box cols of ammunition returned to the sect for transmission to hand cols.	
	5	"	2 Lt Samuel posted to the III sect. having joined the unit from leave on same day	

WAR DIARY
or
INTELLIGENCE SUMMARY.
(Erase heading not required.)

14 STC RFA

Army Form C. 2118

Place	Date	Hour	Summary of Events and Information	Remarks and references to Appendices
	4/10/15	6	2 Lt Sermets parts to #9 Hyper Posta accompd & 1/K.R.R. Lt Johnson RAMC ceases the attack and posts away 6/7 K.R.R. Lt D. Haig RAMC attached as M.O. to the unit	
	11		2 Lt O'Brien & No T sect posts to 7 & 8" Hyper R.F.A	
	14		2 Lt W.R. Clarke posts to this unit from base & posts to No T sect. 2 Lt A. Davis posts to No T sect. 2 Lt Brackley struck off the string & having been evacuated to England	
	21		Horses & space all marks from ammunition wagons & back view coloured dues K.D.Q.O	
	† aug.		2 Lt Peters posts to #6 Hyper & & & & Sergt AF.M.(S.R.) joined this unit game.	

1577 Wt.W10791/1773 500,000 1/15 D.D.&L. A.D.S.S./Forms/C. 2118.

11th Division

14th S.tc.
vol: 3

121/7635

Nov 15

Army Form C. 2118

14. D.A.C - RFA

WAR DIARY
or
INTELLIGENCE SUMMARY.
(Erase heading not required.)

Instructions regarding War Diaries and Intelligence Summaries are contained in F.S. Regs., Part II. and the Staff Manual respectively. Title pages will be prepared in manuscript.

Place.	Date	Hour	Summary of Events and Information	Remarks and references to Appendices
WATOU	1st Nov		Receives 3 complete turnouts from Transport to complete 4 new C.198	
(L10 Aug 28nd 27)	3	"	2.Lt Retin posted to 746 Myrae	
	"	"	2.Lt Schart Posted to DAC	
	11	"	Major A. Burks posted to this unit from #9 Myrae RFA + assumes command of III section. B.S.N. James joined. Fredstrs 1 & seed.	
	15	"	Transpres 1 & 244 mules, equipped with harness from Indian Corps in exchange of horses. Horses were all in very good condition - some were heavy draught.	
	18	"	Major Skelton RSA from No II section to junct to 59" Siege Battery	
	22	"	Capt Risley joined & took over command of II section.	
	28	"	2.Lt Clark attached to 48. Myrae + duty ? 2 Lt & other attached to this unit from 48. Ats in Li strand	
	29	"	30 Ryll draught horses handed over this unit to make up for deficiencies. Heavy draught horses received from Indian Corps. Progress in putting adding rooms joints accommodation during the north glow going to shortage of material. R Es started to help during the last days of the month.	XXX

1577 Wt W10791/1773 500,000 f/15 D.D.&L. A.D.S.S./Forms/C. 2118.

化白 8 月長.
Vol: 4

121/7935

Army Form C. 2118.

WAR DIARY
or
INTELLIGENCE SUMMARY.
(Erase heading not required.)

14 DAC RFA

Place	Date	Hour	Summary of Events and Information	Remarks and references to Appendices
WATOU	5/14/15	1 pm	V.O.'s arrival & Movement Orders of new section (I + II)	
"	6 " "		Receive preliminary orders to prepare to move from II Army area	
"	7 8 9		Remaining horses inoculated, busy negotiating for advance stores, drawing remounts etc	
	9 "		2/Lt Boyd leaves for England. Capt Riley rejoins No II Section	
			2/Lt Jackson returns to No I Section.	
	10.11.12"		Windy, overhauling clothing + equipment + drawing deficiencies	
	13.14.15"		Making up deficiencies + getting wagons repaired	
	17"		2/Lt Clarke rejoins the attacks to S/Sec + rejoins No II Section	
	18		2/Lt Jackson posts from No 2 Sect + No II Sect take over command	
			over Capt Riley. appointed Staff Capt 14 R.A.	
	26		Ordn received cancelling the ordr to withdraw from 2nd Army	
	27		2/Lt Clyfts posts to the column (No 1 Sec)	
	28		2/Lt Colter posts to #9" Bde	
	30		2 Pl O/Min posts to No II Sect	

A/Lt

RETURN.

Amendment to Nominal Rolls rendered you on 19th inst., in accordance with 14th (Light) Division Orders No. 1029 dated 18th inst.

H.V.C.
No. S.E. 6489 Sergeant Walford.

[signature]

In the Field

Capt. R.G.A.
ADJUTANT,
14th DIVISIONAL AMMUN: COL:

[stamp: HD. QRS 14th DIVISIONAL AMMUNITION COLUMN R.F.A. — 21 DEC 1915]

RETURN

Amendment to Nominal Rolls rendered you on 19th inst. in accordance with 14th (Light) Division Routine Orders No 1029 dated 18th inst.

No 38630 Driver Evans of No 2 Section having been evacuated is struck off the strength with effect from 15th inst.

No 96077 Driver Woodward of No 1 Section having been evacuated is struck off strength with effect from 15th inst.

In the Field

Capt. RGA
ADJUTANT,
14th DIVISIONAL AMMUN. COL.

H.Q. 14th DIVISIONAL AMMUNITION COLUMN B.E.F. — 20 DEC 1915

Nominal Roll
Head Quarters 14th Div. Ammn. Column

Regtal. no.	Rank	Name		Remarks
	Lieut. Col.	Birch	A.H.C	
	Captain	Macklow Smith	A	
	Lieut	Haig	D	
52123	R.S.M.	Barrett	W.	
43205	B.Q.M.S	Adams	C.B.	
22435	Sergt.	Hammick	P.B.	
41684	A/Bdr.	Cassidy	E	
32132	Gunner	Abell	A	
88434	"	Bell	A.S.	
12181	"	Brodie	J	
5925	"	Butcher	E.J.	
24582	"	Carthew	J.J.	
51540	"	Hunt	J.H	
1347	"	Leech	J.S.	
70404	"	Nelson	A.	
33512	"	Shaw	J	
3461	"	Shearing	W	
95413	"	Storey	A.R	
95965	"	Wilson	J.A	
81664	Driver	Bishop	W.R	
72468	"	Cooke	E.W.	
93819	"	Easedale		
90049	"	Halfyard	H	
343	"	Hume	S	
60210	"	New	G.	
72434	"	Masshedar	A	
95045	"	Priest	P.H	
33340	"	Southern	W	
72504	"	Taylor	B.W	
72806	"	Thistle	W	
72299	"	Swells	A	
95401	"	Wood	A	

19/XII/15

Nominal Roll of No, Section 1st D.A.Column R.F.A.

Regt'l No	Rank & Name	Remarks	Regt'l No	Rank & Name	Remarks
	Capt Stewart J.S	On Leave	34418	Gnr Field W.W.	
	Lieut Shard C.B.		84929	- Forbester J	
	2/Lt Penrose J		115308	- Gilroy W	Cavalry Discharge
			3861	- Hacklin R	
15385	BSM James G.H		59116	- Foster E.C	attd Hd Qrs
34695	Sgt Faulkner E.P		72487	- Hart P	
32327	- Parker H		95784	- Higgins L	attd Hd Qrs
39845	Bm Sgt Hood H		95785	- Holbourne A	attd Hd Qrs
21244	Corpl Brazell J		97775	- Humphries J	
99771	- Marshall W		21603	- Johnson S	
64210	- Knight L.W		3802	- Lewis T	
84723	- Jones J		89840	- King A	
51878	Bdr SS Vokins H		104201	- Lynch J	
90164	- Linis R		93632	- Helmes A	
39175	Bdr Hyde A.J		99760	- Ollerenshaw G	
59187	- Ames L.V	attd R.T.O Caustre	20108	- Robinson G	
96486	- Cooke C.R		99883	- Rowntree D	
236	- Stewart J		21808	- Sawyers W	Hospital
49372	- Walmsley T		63224	- Self H.C	
62971	- Hewitt J		88665	- Timms J.S	
21817	Bdr Trigg A.C		97082	- Trehearne E.L	
64878	- Corcoran P		15626	- Washbrooke J	
72453	- Wright S		71591	- Wattam A	attd 46 B.A.C.
72770	- Chappell H.S				
63621	- Hebden H				
59021	Gnr Bale H.G		52607	SS Cairns A	
21313	- Balderson F		72769	- Cherry J	attd Hd Qrs
27444	- Bratly J		98316	- Hood H	
41230	- Cameron J		90182	- Hennell G.H	
59151	- Cook J				
64877	- Corcoran J				
59974	- Cox A.J.H		02333	Wh'r Rickhouse G	
99304	- Dalrymple		90339	Saddler Harrison G.P	
7275	- Eves P		68969	- (Proby) Reed W	

Reg'l No	Rank & name	Remarks	Reg'l No	Rank & name	Remarks
72406	D'. Abbey J.T.		60014	D'. Connor S.	
80822	- Alexander H		72668	- Cotterill R	
72407	- Allan W.A		59128	- Cotton G	
72405	- Arnott L.O		27354	- Currie D.	
27118	- Aspey H		98042	- Cuss A.E.	
99271	- Barrass C		72473	- Dalton T	
72662	- Beech C		72772	- Darby A	
27472	- Bingham C.S	Hospital	57914	- Dickens T.E	
6176	- Borthwick W.		72516	- Dowson W	
89388	- Bostock C		79184	- Durkin C	
90360	- Bousefield G		21574	- Eglantine T	
72764	- Bradley G		2797	- Elder W	S.R. awaiting Discharge
58979	- Brine F.		27053	- Fieldhouse A	
59228	- Broadway J		97419	- Fuller V.	
72413	- Brooksbank R		82296	- Garnett W.	
64859	- Brown L.		72779	- Gower H	
72414	- Buckland C.E	Hospital	94880	- Gridley J.	
95743	- Burbridge T		72485	- Hall J.	
34922	- Burke J		34431	- Hardy J.W	
90286	- Burke Jn		72784	- Hartshorne T	
20721	- Butler G		80610	- Heard R.	Hospital
34923	- Cammiss J.W		27047	- Holmes J.	D°
58961	- Carliss E.		72783	- Honey W	
72419	- Carrick C.H		102827	- Hunt E	
27310	- Carter M		72432	- Ireland J.A.	
72420	- Chapman S		95831	- Jobling F	
73367	- Clinch F.		60113	- Joyce J.	
64938	- Codd H.W.		73139	- Kightley T.R	
72418	- Conlon A		80360	- Leigh J.H.	
34927	- Conlon T.		91662	- Lock H	

Regt No	Rank & Name	Remarks	Regt No	Rank & Name	Remarks
93213	P. Lillie H		72452	P. White C.S.	
37822	- Tunstall A		95749	- Whitehouse J	
14888	- Morgan T		72809	- Winterburn R	
72438	- Medhem J		93560	- Wilson J	
72796	- Oliphant J		64355	- Wilson R	
96054	- Parkin W		72403	- Woodward A	
72440	- Parkinson E		96077	- Woodward D	Hospital
22404	- Pegler A		80100	- Wormald A	
59686	- Pidgeon E.J	Hospital	84811	- Wright J.T	
51810	- Poynton H		72396	- Wilson T	
17039	- Randall W				
10176	- Rathbone				
72444	- Scott C				
80820	- Simmons G				
80608	- Smith J				
63849	- Snowdon H				
80617	- Sprattles S				
72804	- Stephenson W				
73141	- Stevenson W.H				
72445	- Sykes A				
72449	- Taylor H				
72389	- Townsend C				
83919	- Turner H.J				
72480	- Tranmer T				
84831	- Turnbull G				
96071	- Turnbull J.W				
72402	- Walker T				
93590	- Watson A				
45343	- West W				
72404	- Whelan T				

Nominal Roll of No. II Section - 14th. D.A.C.   19/12/15.

REG'MT. No.	RANK	NAME	REMARKS
	2/Lieut.	E. S. Jackson. R.F.A.	
	2/Lieut.	W. R. Clarke. R.F.A.	
	2/Lieut.	H. B. Davis. R.F.A.	
44585.	B.S.M.	Robinson, G.H.	
83744	Sergeant	Lloyd, R.	
	"	Dalton, B.G.	
2407	Sergt.(A.V.C)	Maddams, H.	
6334	Farr. Sergt.	Dickerson, F.	
67442	Corporal	Greig, J.W.	
90371	"	Illingworth, F.	
88687	"	Fram, J.R.	
31490	"	Perrins, B.A.	
68801	Corpl. S.S.	Gow, F.	
27157	Bombdr.	Bell, J.R.	
45538	"	Copsey, A.	
72650	"	Staniland, A.L.	
58889	"	Broxton, W.H.	
89536	"	Spurrier, W.	
21809	"	Shaw, E.G.	
72585	A/Bomdr.	Huddlestone, J.H.	
44332	"	Mellor, J.A.	
70253	"	Rafferty, J.	
69036	"	Sharpe, H.	
84627	"	Fisher, E.	
10784	S.S/Bombr.	Roberts, W.	
98150	"	Alexander, W.	
27209	"	Barr, G.	
72617	"	Blinkhorn, H.	
72499	"	Smith, R.	
78835	"	Briggs, J.	
34419	"	Gilbert, H.	

90156	Shoeing Smith	Boatfield, N.
106120	"	Burgess, J.E.
72583	"	Goodfellow, H.
17529	"	Draper, J.D.
58888	Fitter	Bates, G.A.
73010	Saddler	Kidger, C.
31540	"	Horsey, J.
44588	Gunner	Anderson, H.
72763	"	Bainbridge, J.
58954	"	Batham, J.D.
58996	"	Bauckham, W.
27138	"	Bell, J.H.
50634	"	Blacka, R.
89284	"	Bradley, J.
90004	"	Brown, J.
59219	"	Brown, W.L.
58948	"	Burry, J.
27463	"	Charlesworth, J.
27568	"	Collins, C.
72465	"	Esgate, J.A.
72646	"	Fawcett, C.
72918	"	Fearn, A.
72578	"	Flower, J.
80330	"	Lock, A.
51725	"	O'bee, E.
103830	"	Leven, W.
72538	"	Peck, W.H.
45334	"	Seedhouse, S.
86331	"	Smith, A.
44479	"	Topliss, E.E.
76128	"	Turner, J.
89182	"	Wilson, H.
34928	"	Woodroffe

21820	Gunner	Wright. J.E.
35725	"	Reynolds. G.
5261	"	Leather. A.
56030	"	Heard. R.A.
83571	Driver	Alcock. J.
27071	"	Allason. J.C.
58174	"	Almond. S.R.
90358	"	Alvey. S.
27060	"	Anderson. J.
83972	"	Andrews. A.
72461	"	Antliff. C.
34443	"	Armitage. F.
97801	"	Atlee. G.
27063	"	Ashurst. J.W.
59178	"	Bartlett. J.B.
72613	"	Barton. W.
84834	"	Bean. J.
21617	"	Bee. C.
72466	"	Bell. H.
21514	"	Bell. G.
21515	"	Bell. W.
58987	"	Bone. A.S.
27826	"	Boulby. H.
72762	"	Bradley. J.
34620	"	Brailey. G.
72561	"	Broadbent. R.
27125	"	Bullcock. H.
72612	"	Burchly. H.
27229	"	Burt. J.
61783	"	Caddick. A.
90458	"	Campbell. J.
72742	"	Catton. F.

64846	Driver	Chiverton, G.	
88934	"	Collins, F.H.	
72621	"	Cooke, J.W.	
72476	"	Cooper, H.	
83946	"	Cox, W.J.	
102896	"	Chatters, A.G.	
72571	"	Duncan, N.	
96491	"	Duthoit, C.	
43994	"	Edwards, J.	
83683	"	Evans, W.	
72596	"	Fenwick, W.	
42946	"	Fottrell, C.	
81632	"	Freeman, A.	
72582	"	Gibbon, R.	
83631	"	Gibbs, J.	
72678	"	Green, J.E.	
83578	"	Hadley, J.	
89519	"	Hawker, W.P.	
83641	"	Hawthorne, H.	
72584	"	Haywood, D.	
72223	"	Hodgson, C.	
62216	"	Holliday, W.	
83766	"	Hooper, A.	
84062	"	Hunt, H.	
17016	"	Hunt, J.	
89022	"	Howell, J.W.	
99021	"	Humphries, J.C.	
95660	"	James, C.	
72282	"	Jenkins, W.H.	
42586	"	Jennison, W.	
96026	"	Johnston, J.	
72588	"	Kendall, A.	
84056	"	Kennett, S.	

72489	Driver	Kirby. H.	
72530	"	Knowles. J.	
21524	"	Lamb. C.	
23334	"	Logan, A.	
21662	"	Lort, J.	
85048	"	Law. W.	
83846	"	Marsh J.	
72592	"	Marshall	
60193	"	Mead, A.	
60225	"	McKibbons W.	
106409	"	Mitchell T.J.D.	
106473	"	McDonald C.C.	
65668	"	Murphy. T.	
84794	"	Mason T.	
90629	"	Matthews	
68804	"	Peacock. C.W.	
102804	"	Pocock G	
72745	"	Pattison J	
35153	"	Redman	
72748	"	Riches. G.	
49443	"	Robilliard L	
72752	"	Seymour E.	
88747	"	Sheahan J.	
89415	"	Smith J	
72387	"	Smith W M.	
72652	"	Spencer H.	
33369	"	Stanley J. L	
83949	"	Talbot G.	
99762	"	Thompson C.W.	
72503	"	Thompson H.	
102926	"	Thrussel W.	
51885	"	Tipple J.	
79891	"	Vernon H	

79892	Driver	Vernon, W. H.	
72658	"	Waterworth. W.	
45214	"	Webster. L.	
72808	"	Wheelocker. G.	
72809	"	Wood. C.	
72608	"	Whitehead. C.	
72759	"	Wilcock. C. F. P.	
81662	"	Williams. H.	
	"	Morris	

Nominal Roll

3rd Section 14th D.A.C

Reg'tl No.	Rank	Name		Reg'tl No.	Rank	Name	
–	Major	Butler	A.I.R.	86338	Saddler	Maycock	H.J.W.
–	Lieut	Hughes	M.McK.	3195	Cpl. Wheeler	Duxfield	T.
–	2nd Lieut	Taylor	W.C.	72514	Fitter	Clark	W.
15170	B.S.M.	Roberts	S.H.	60218	S/a Bom	Armstrong	G.
44811	Sergeant	Harvey	J.	22352	"	Allen	A.
46669	"	Childs-Satchell	A.E.	83814	Gunner	Barrow	H.
59164	Corporal	Lawson	A.A.	45291	"	Banks	A.
96270	"	Rogers	J.	21610	"	Bushnell	G.
81687	"	Slater	W.	34925	"	Barker	R.
62987	"	Wright	T.	22415	"	Barker	E.
18840	Bomb.	Gaywood	C.	60175	"	Bouquet	H.
83916	"	Jones	B.	33037	"	Cooper	D.H.
33564	"	Mills	H.	89007	"	Field	W.
21534	"	Nutter	R.	22423	"	Harwood	J.
20511	"	Smith	L.	20083	"	Hodgetts	T.
60235	a/Bom	Cooksey	W.	96475	S/a Bom	Jackson	J.
70397	"	Henshaw	J.	104194	Gunner	Kerrigan	W.
60176	"	Jeffrey	S.B.	2847	"	Larkin	T.
20100	"	Smith	C.W.	108688	"	Lees	E.
22434	"	Weston	G.A.	71446	"	Lee	J.
2278	A.V.C Sergt	Maddams	C.	110812	"	Laws	W.
98618	Far Sergt	Knight	A.	103778	"	Gilmour	W.
7131	Corp S.S.	Davies	J.	88515	"	Trohan	J.
90150	S. Smith	Barrett	A.	99113	"	Marshall	G.
60102	"	Fretwell	J.W.	83908	"	Morris	J.
98564	"	McNamara	P.	7786	S/a Bom	McCann	W.J.
95941	"	Parker	G.	88707	Gunner	McCarthy	A.
32719	Saddler	Busid	H.	89641	"	McGrath	E.

Reg number	Rank	Name		Reg No	Rank	Name	
50641	Gunner	Tennet	B	98057	Driver	Lloyd	W.
36261	S/a Bom	Peace	A	22410	"	Francis	W.
17420	Gunner	Rainbow	A.	69239	"	Gould	H.
95950	"	Snape	H.	47495	"	Gardner	G.
35193	"	Sutcliffe	E.	90516	"	Gittens	W.
19408	"	Surplice	E.	23771	"	Geary	T
87819	"	Seymour	H.	49946	"	Gilbert	A.
35196	"	Watts	A.	88951	"	Hennessy	H.
80791	"	Wallington	W.	34213	"	Hickson	T
79849	"	Wilkinson	B	10582	"	Holland	W
50638	"	Whittaker	H.	83606	S/a Bom	Howard	E.
89792	"	White	JH	6661	Driver	Ingram	J
9507	"	Webb	E.	36249	"	Ingham	S.
89307	Driver	Adshead	H.	89598	"	Jenkins	W.
46946	"	Bazley	G.	88864	"	Jennings	W.S.
6694	"	Boyle	J.	96527	"	Jobling	T
27225	"	Brown	J.E.	102823	"	Kirkham	W
28236	"	Crouch	S	89226	"	Kelteridge	W.
67389	"	Christopher	E	23600	"	Kingsland	W.G.
23763	"	Campbell	D	96211	"	Lambert	W
46470	"	Casey	J	22439	"	List	E
46471	"	Clayton	W.	81489	"	Lowry	J
46472	"	Cunningham	H	81490	"	Liversidge	J
97970	S/a Bom	Cook	R.	100299	"	Larmour	J
47496	Driver	Craig	R.	6120	"	McKeown	B
43998	"	Cheshire	T	72793	"	Moffat	W
84000	"	Cope	L.	85824	"	Monks	J
60679	S/a Bom	Drake	J	12164	"	Mullett	W.
22429	Driver	Fenson	A	47152	"	May	T
6181	"	Fiddes	D.	48988	"	Morgan	W.J.
23187	"	Feeney	J	72792	"	Mark	W

Reg N°	Rank	Name		Reg N°	Rank	Name	
98049	Driver	Maslin	J	90515	Driver	Rolls	H.
81715	"	Mander	H	102885	"	Snedker	H
90513	"	Mason	L.	49498	"	Simpson	W
59963	"	Moffat	M	23247	"	Stewart	G.
88703	"	McClelland	H	88996	"	Steele	W.
47490	"	McGilvray	A	89011	"	Shaw	A
60196	"	Merrington	A	20068	"	Terry	J.
46493	"	Miller	S	21555	"	Tidswell	A.
83909	"	Moles	P.	22418	"	Tibble	C.
23761	"	Murphy	A	83924	"	Tucker	W.H.
83742	"	Munn	J	89742	"	Wallington	S.
90512	"	McGuire	J	60213	"	Wright	J.
59959	"	Nibló	T	48357	S/o Bom	Worsley	H.
98166	"	Nutt	L.	10469	Driver	Westwood	R
18572	"	O'Rourke	P	10729	"	Wilcox	H
34405	"	O'Brien	P.	96110	"	Wilson	J.
118451	"	Penton	H	33595	"	West	C.
1601	"	Penfold	A.H.	12606	"	Wilkinson	R.
88915	"	Pallett	C.				
90511	"	Parker	S.				
12797	S/o Bom	Parry	W.H.				
83748	"	Phillips	A.				
59742	Driver	Pearson	H.				
6666	"	Peoples	W.J.				
40163	"	Pye	T.				
83900	"	Punce	A				
89246	"	Price	H				
6320	"	Rice	D				
93111	"	Robertson	G.				
6175	"	Robertson	G.G.				
10826	"	Rugman	V.C.				

14 P. S. A.
2 Pl. 5
Pan 16.

Army Form C. 2118.

WAR DIARY
or
INTELLIGENCE SUMMARY.
(Erase heading not required.)

1 A.D.A.C. - PFA

Instructions regarding War Diaries and Intelligence Summaries are contained in F. S. Regs., Part II. and the Staff Manual respectively. Title pages will be prepared in manuscript.

Place	Date	Hour	Summary of Events and Information	Remarks and references to Appendices
WATOU	4/1/16	—	Handed over 25" wagon (infantry) for fatigues from Moerbeke + sent them to Remount Depot. Have 1 Tent & No II section. Position of Remount awaited. A Column to move from the hutt.	
		9.—	All wagons the matins went a Divisional hutt.	
		12. 30.	Moved the new camp AR at A12.d11 sheet 27 Poll The I section occupies camp Syndelou while No III section went to A24a49 sheet 27 the Advanced section. New camp was vacated of 43" Division some left in a very dirty & insanitary condition. Battery of infantrymen orderlies clearing the hutts. This ADS was attached to Chief of divisional fatigues. No lads sent in on its camp to caretaker of 20° Div An. Col.	

[signature]

Army Form C. 2118.

WAR DIARY
or
INTELLIGENCE SUMMARY.
(Erase heading not required.)

14 D.A.C. R.F.A.

Place	Date	Hour	Summary of Events and Information	Remarks and references to Appendices
St. SIXTE	1st July 1916		Occupied the day in cleaning up camp & improving the accommodation	
	2 – 5		2/Lt Davis posted. French Indian bathing. Improving & cleaning camp & carrying out fatigue duty for R.E.'s	
	6		C.R.A. inspects camp & horses.	
	9		Received orders to withdraw from the present position to 2nd Army Area near CASSEL	
	10		Informed that 20 D.A.C. would take over present line on 13th inst.	
	12		Self advanced party to take over camping area Hellette J.20.8.9. at and near ARNEKE (H24) hrs. Start 27	
	13		Busy packing waggons & company known as 14th at 7 am	
	14		Marched to camping area by 20 D.A.C. near ARNEKE via WATOU, HOUTKERQUE, HERZEELE, WORMHOUDT & LEDRINGHEM a total distance of about 19 miles. Arrived in billets at about 3 p.m.	
	15-16		Cleaning down waggons & packing up ammunition. Taken over from 20 D.A.C.	
	17		Ammunition Park & transport left by train for night billet	
	22		Entrained in 5 trains from CASSEL & ESQUELBECQ for LONGAU near	

WAR DIARY
or
INTELLIGENCE SUMMARY.

Army Form C. 2118.

Place	Date	Hour	Summary of Events and Information	Remarks and references to Appendices
LIGNEREUIL			Where are the ammunition of N.III sent was dumped under the charge of an Offr. The Wagons & Limbers returned to the D.A.C. to be built up being available at LIGNEREUIL they built up at BLAVINCOURT a village about ½ mile away	
BEAUVAL	25"		Capt. Stewart returns from ENGLAND & reports him arrival. He also brought a draught of 2 Offrs & 20 mm of 4.5" Artillery.	AVCVBrich LH

WAR DIARY or INTELLIGENCE SUMMARY

Army Form C. 2118.

14 D A C – RFA

Place	Date	Hour	Summary of Events and Information	Remarks and references to Appendices
ST VASTE	23		AMIENS. Snowing all the time & froze hard during the night. Marched to billets at ST VASTE, last section arriving at abt 3 p.m.	
	24		Received orders at 8.45 a.m. to march to billets at BEAUVAL at 9 a.m. Arrived BEAUVAL at abt 4 p.m. Found the town very full & great difficulty experienced in getting billets.	
	25		Orders to march to ETREE WAMIN at 2.15 p.m. Frost continued & snow rather deep, still snowing. Roads were very bad for horses. H.Q. arrived at DOULLENS at abt 7 p.m. & found no billets available in town. Got some accommodation in Petroleum-y town & some at BRETELL. Paid J. No III sect & a few waggons of No I sect & left in at abt 1 a.m. Det. unknown rear No III sect lost & remain in road. Commenced to Raw. No 9 & No 1 proceeded to ETREE WAMIN during the afternoon & No III sect arrived next day, also No II section.	
	26			
	27		remained at billets	
	28		orders to march to LIGNEREUIL & billetts with 48 Bde R.F.A. No III sect went to BERNEVILLE to establish an Ammunition Depot	

Army Form C. 2118.

14 D.A.C. - R.F.A

WAR DIARY
or
INTELLIGENCE SUMMARY.
(Erase heading not required.)

Instructions regarding War Diaries and Intelligence Summaries are contained in F. S. Regs., Part II. and the Staff Manual respectively. Title pages will be prepared in manuscript.

Place	Date	Hour	Summary of Events and Information	Remarks and references to Appendices
LINGEREUIL BARLY	March 1916 1st–16th		Remained in Billets at LINGEREUIL & BAVINCOURT	
	6	11 am	Previous two billets at BARLY - made very satisfactory - nothing unusual to report.	
HAUTEVILLE	19th	11.30	Previous two billets at HAUTEVILLE. H.Q. Billets at Chateau - the men were housed in the Bruel Huts. HAUTEVILLE was taken over from the French the left at their own billets in a very dirty + unsanitary condition.	
to			Nothing unusual to report. The column has no front line small arm ammunition & sends about 30 wagon a day to draw some of M.S.C. from Raie Gas.	
	31st		Nothing unusual went except that an amount at HAUTEVILLE no arrangements was made to existed for watering horses, we had to water at LATTRE ST QUENTIN & on this two H. 5th Div area commenced difficulties arose which are not yet settled.	

A.W.Birch Lt Col

WAR DIARY or INTELLIGENCE SUMMARY

Army Form C. 2118.

14 DAC. R.F.A. Vol 8

Place	Date	Hour	Summary of Events and Information	Remarks and references to Appendices
APRIL				
HAUTEVILLE	4th		S.A. Ammunition returns this gave us 6 empties waggon teams for horse returns & horse on tr to 4"DAC, to 1/2 ESSAC	
"	5th		91 & 6" DAC. Lus from 4" DAC were returned.	
"	6th		Nr Conrad Lu. Athon Paget, Lt. 6. Cpl. Artillery Commander inspected the Livers & Willetts & made some recommendations for improvements in how lines etc.	
"	7th		Capt Stewart attached 546 Hav. employment as a B.C.	
"	8th		Capt Haig R.A.M.C. Gentle Crane RB relieved by Cl Hart R.A.M.C.	
"	10		The Adjutant went to ARRAS to get some chaff cutters. He promised to send the repaired ones & get them in charge.	
	10		Sgt Sweeteman grants 1 month leave on condition his B. enjoys a complete 21 years. Q.M.S. ADAMS grants leave under same condition for the 7th mile.	
	13		We leave Shopper & all ranks in leave orders begin the units. The G.O.C. 14 Div with C.R.A. inspected hour lines that of the units. ADVS inspected No III Section Lines & cart available & 26 Mobile Vet Section	

Army Form C. 2118.

WAR DIARY
or
INTELLIGENCE SUMMARY.   14 D.A.C - RFA
(Erase heading not required.)

Instructions regarding War Diaries and Intelligence Summaries are contained in F.S. Regs., Part II. and the Staff Manual respectively. Title pages will be prepared in manuscript.

Place	Date	Hour	Summary of Events and Information	Remarks and references to Appendices
HAUTVILLE	25"	12 Noon	3rd Army the Commander inspects Horse lines of unit	
"	"		Lt Stanals proceeds on leave	
"	28		Drew 54 Mules (remounts) stands nos 30 & 15 horse to brigade.	
"	29		C.R.A visits the unit	
"	30		A.D.V.S inspects all horses of the column. He was pleased with the general state of no III section horses but found the no II section horses were suffering from the excessive fatigue of last winter while at WATOU.	

Auersmith
Lt Colonel
Cmdg 14 D.A.C

1577   Wt. W10791/1773   500,000   1/15   D. D. & L.   A.D.S.S./Forms/C. 2118.

Vol 9
14 D.A.C - R.F.A

WAR DIARY or INTELLIGENCE SUMMARY

Place	Date	Hour	Summary of Events and Information	Remarks and references to Appendices
HAUTEVILLE	MAY 1916 10th		The Lt. Col Commanding Proceeded on leave from 10th to 19th. Major Brookbank assumes Command	
	12		The C.R.A Inspects the horses of all the section	
	18		Received notification that the D.A.C was to be reorganized from a H.Q. & two echelons "A" & "B". A Echelon to form 5 each of the 47, 48 & 49 B.A.Cs the 46 B.A.C being broken up to complete the 47, 48 & 49; N.C.O.s in their new formations called Section 1.2 & 3 respectively the "B" Echelon also to be formed one in each of the D.A.C. and called No 4 Section	
	21st		The new formation & organization came into effect; C/M Wost [Wostenholm?] relieved by C.M. Vezenett[?]	
	26		Our Surplus stores & one vehicle now used by horse to ABBEVILLE there was 1 waggon 76 horses 107 N.C.O.s. Same they were entrained by M. Holmes & by Beakton who returned by rail	
	30		Returned our surplus harness & stores to Romance [?]	
	31		Returned our surplus waggons (23) + wheresoft [?] (3) which we loaded on to the R.T.O at SAVY station the G.O.C of the Brigade inspected all the horses of the D.A.C arrangement just	

14 DAC. RFA
Vol 10. June

WAR DIARY
INTELLIGENCE SUMMARY

Place	Date	Hour	Summary of Events and Information	Remarks and references to Appendices
HAUTVILLE	1st June 19/16		The Corps Commander inspected us. He knew of the StC and expressed his satisfaction with their condition.	
	2nd		8 letters home went on leave.	
	3rd		Two conscription Remounts (Rees for the 5th division) proceeded to KNABEVILLE by Route to report to new Commandant.	
	4th		Drawn for all centres who have been in the country 12 months inwards.	
	5th		to 8 pm Day for the whole column. 2/Lt Major H. Robinson of No. 2 Section proceeds to A/49 Bde.	
	14		Adopted Summer Office time. At 11pm all clocks were advanced one hour.	
	21		C.R.A inspects Horses + camps of the 4 Section.	
	23		2/Lt Hughes returns from leave.	
	24		Major Brochabade proceeds home to join K.W.O. Brings the HQ. Officers to Berneville. Received now opening.	
			BERNEVILLE as a temporary measure.	
	26.		G.1092.275 — Received to Remounts for Column. Sgt Major Kelly of No 2 Section granted a Commission in R.F.A and posted to 37th Division	
	30.		Received orders to the prepared to move three batteries at GOUVES at short notice. Inspects	

WAR DIARY
or
INTELLIGENCE SUMMARY.   14 D.A.C. R.F.A

Army Form C. 2118.

Place	Date	Hour	Summary of Events and Information	Remarks and references to Appendices
BERNEVILLE	June 30"		He (units ans additions) them 4th section same day.	
			[signature] Lt Colonel Commanding 14 D.A.C.	

ORIGINAL

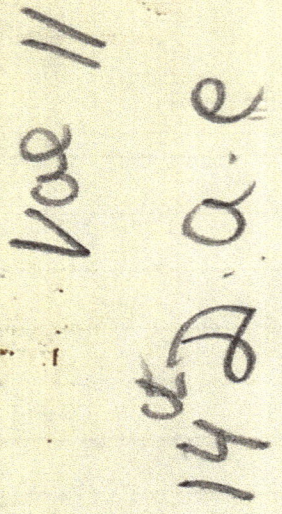

CONFIDENTIAL
================

WAR DIARY

OF

14TH DIVISIONAL AMMUNITION COLUMN

From 1st July 1916.   To 31st July 1916.

=*=*=*=*=*=*=*=

(Volume 15)

Original
Army Form C. 2118.

14 DAC - RFA

WAR DIARY
or
INTELLIGENCE SUMMARY.
(Erase heading not required.)

Instructions regarding War Diaries and Intelligence Summaries are contained in F. S. Regs., Part II. and the Staff Manual respectively. Title pages will be prepared in manuscript.

Place	Date	Hour	Summary of Events and Information	Remarks and references to Appendices
BERNEVILLE	JULY			
	1		Received Report on Coys Commander inspection of S.H.Cs	
	3		"A" C.B. SHARP received orders to proceed England report to W.O.	
	5		Yhe C.O. and Adjutant returned into Office from ather BERNEVILLE to HAUTVILLE. Capt. McCulloch of No 3 Sect. appointed town major at BERNEVILLE.	
HAUTEVILLE	6 & 6		Drawing stores ammunition grenades etc & advance stores from MONTENESCOURT and locality which were left by 5 Div. Artillery.	
	10		2 N.C.Os. & 5 drivers left the column to a maximum hundred Battery	
	14		Reinforcements one battalion of 1st division arrived at HAUTVILLE.	
	15		Recommended to dump 150 Rds per gun of 18 pr + 100 Rds per gun of 4.5 How.	
	17		4 N.C.Os. & men left for Heavy Hand Hotchkiss School	
	9"		Received 9 remounts (mules)	
	18"		2/Lt EASTWOOD was transferred to 55" Div. Artillery & 2/Lt W.L. BEARENS of 55" Div Artly joins this unit & proceeds to the same. 2/Lt W.L. Hughes joins the 2 section.	
	21		Lt Hughes joins the 2 section. Also some Spirits & horse shoes for the Column. C.R.A. inspects the Turnout.	

Original

Army Form C. 2118.

14 DAC. RFA

WAR DIARY
or
INTELLIGENCE SUMMARY.
(Erase heading not required.)

Place	Date	Hour	Summary of Events and Information	Remarks and references to Appendices
HAUTVILLE	22 July		A.D.V.S. arranged transport home of No 4 Section. He did not arrive.	
	28		C.R.A. inspects horse lines of No 4 Section & HQ's.	
			Lt Jackson & Lt W.C. Taylor returned tho 4 Sect. from being attached to Brigades for instruction.	
	30		Nos 4 Section with the S.A.A portion of A Echelon attacked proceeds to Pont Thard to INERGNY to accompany the division; the remaining 14 Div. Artillery being attached to 21st division temporarily.	
	29		2/Lt Behrens was attached to No 1 Sect.	

Ainsworth
Lt Colonel
Cmdg. 14 AFC

CONFIDENTIAL

WAR DIARY

OF

14TH DIVISIONAL AMMUNITION COLUMN

From 1st August.   To 31st August.

(VOLUME XVl)

Confidential

Staff Capt. R.A.
    14th Div.

[Stamp: HD QRS 14th DIVISION / 2 SEP 1916 / AMMUNITION COLUMN R.F.A.]

Herewith War Diary for the Month of August for this Column.
Please acknowledge receipt.

2.9.16

Shackleton
Capt R.A.
Adjt. 14 DAC

Army Form C. 2118.

WAR DIARY
or
INTELLIGENCE SUMMARY.   14 DAC—RFA

(Erase heading not required.)

Instructions regarding War Diaries and Intelligence Summaries are contained in F.S. Regs., Part II. and the Staff Manual respectively. Title pages will be prepared in manuscript.

Place	Date	Hour	Summary of Events and Information	Remarks and references to Appendices
HAUTVILLE	4	9.30	HQ 14 Echelon moves from HAUTEVILLE by Route march to LUCHEUX & BELLETS	
	5	—	Continued march to BOISBERGUE when we joined up with 4th Section	
	6	—	Rested in Billets at BOISBERGUE & reorganised into & normal organisation	
	7	—	Marches to NAOURS where we billeted the night	
	8	—	Continued march to camp & arrived near here crossing 1/4 mile N.W. B DERNANCOURT. We arrived at about 11 p.m. after a 24 mile march. No has the connection & horses during the march.	
	9 & 10		Rests in camp & taken dump from 51st D.A.C. at E.11.d.8.8. Took over from 51st D.A.C. at E.16.a central (Sheet 62 D)	
			Drawing ammunition from Rail Head & dumping at dump Drawing Supplies from Rail Head & delivering to dump	
MEAULTE	11			
	12			
	13			
	14 to 22		Continuing to supply ammunition from Rail Head to Dump & to from Dump to the XV Corps rendering great assistance. The daily number of rounds of average 11,000 A, 3000 Ax & 3500 Bx about. During this period we have moved 16 horses though & replace casualties & 1 18/pr ammunition body.	

1577   Wt.W10791/1773   500,000   1/15   D.D. & L.   A.D.S.S./Forms/C. 2118.

Army Form C. 2118.

WAR DIARY
or
INTELLIGENCE SUMMARY. 14 D.A.C - R.F.A

(Erase heading not required.)

Instructions regarding War Diaries and Intelligence Summaries are contained in F.S. Regs., Part II. and the Staff Manual respectively. Title pages will be prepared in manuscript.

Place	Date	Hour	Summary of Events and Information	Remarks and references to Appendices
	August 1916			
MEAULTE	23/24		Nothing of importance to report. Three surplus horses formerly Simcoe wagon Horse Transport depot. ABBEVILLE returned. Horse strength now strength. Two mules of No 2 sect were killed by shrapnel whilst conveying T.M. stores to amm. dump. 47 Hong No 1 sect was killed while feeding empty shell cases from Gun Position.	
	25		A G.G.C.M. was assembled at H.Q. 14 Divn by order of G.O.C. 14 Divn. For the trial of 2/Lt A.S.H TAYLOR & Lieut Gordon Notting & Lt. W. CHIDWICK 146 M.G. The latter was acquitted. Lt. EASTWOOD reported his arrival on being posted from the 55 S.R. 2/Lt BEHRENS returns to return to 55 S.R.	
	27			
	31"		Steel helmets were issued, complete issue of 1 per man.	

cwmsmith
Lt Colonel

1577 Wt.W10791/1773 500,000 1/15 D. D. & L. A.D.S.S./Forms/C. 2118.

ORIGINAL

CONFIDENTIAL

WAR DIARY

OF

14TH DIVISIONAL AMM. COL.

FOR.

SECPTEMBER 1916.

VOLUME XV11.

WAR DIARY
INTELLIGENCE SUMMARY. 14 D.A.C - R.F.A.

Army Form C. 2118.

Place	Date	Hour	Summary of Events and Information	Remarks and references to Appendices
MEAULTE	September 1916 1-2ᵈ		Nothing of importance to record – Ammunition supply normal.	
"		3ʳᵈ	10 mules were killed by shell at MAMETZ while outwards from the DAC to convoy loads up for 24 DAC.	
		9ᵗʰ	2/Lt O'Brien & 2/Lieut Reiver posted to H.Q: Brigade vice 2/Lt Dyke & 2/Lt Stanley Welsh posted to this unit from H.Q: Brigade. Capt Lamois attached to H.Q: Brigade.	
		"	New Zealand D.A.C took over from 33 D.A.C. & works in co-operation with this unit.	
		6ᵗʰ		
		7ᵗʰ	Received 54 mules as remounts & horses nos 27 from & Brigade following day.	
		13ᵗʰ	The Adjutant went to FRICOURT & selected site for the dump and A Echelon.	
		14	at 7am B Echelon & all G.S. wagons from A Echelon took over dump at BECORDEL and encamped at E 12 ℓ (map sheet 57c) Capt Alexander moves forward from a new advances dump at FRICOURT at F4 c 88. H.Q. & A Echelon encamped near to FRICOURT at F4 Central.	
		15	2 advanced sections of N.Z. D.A.C arrived and encamped next to us at about 10 am.	
		17	H.Q. and Ams! Section moved to new position near MONTAUBAN in the valley	

WAR DIARY or INTELLIGENCE SUMMARY

14 DAC - RFA

Army Form C. 2118.

Place	Date	Hour	Summary of Events and Information	Remarks and references to Appendices
MONTAUBAN	17th Sept.		Move the advance dump which was formed the previous night at S21d99 nearer Section N.3 the encamps in S21a. All 14 S.A. wagon lines in N.3. Battery encamped on the approx. ground.	
	17		at about 11 am transferred ammunition dump to S22a under cover of the high ground the w/ slight of enemy observation balloon. Enemy commence shelling the camps with HE. at about 11 pm weather lets up remained here.	
	18		very wet all day. Ground impossible to lorries. Enemy harass the w/r. was shelling all day & night. Raid Section tried to move camp to S27a & S27c. HQ remains but left next morning remncamps S27a.11 still dirty wet. Enemy harass range & shell roads blowing up an ammunition lorry near on camp.	
	19		No.4 Section (M Sclater) moves to camp in A4b with h.q. [producing?] Bcolm. Road leas so the watericels at A9b let ammunit train his w/s arrive & lorris brought ammo to RICOURT dump from where it to the cartel by M Sclater hoas dump.	
	20		Moves ammunition dump to A2b39 in the morning and lyd ammunition	

Army Form C. 2118.

WAR DIARY
or
INTELLIGENCE SUMMARY.
(Erase heading not required.)

Place	Date	Hour	Summary of Events and Information	Remarks and references to Appendices
MONTAUBAN.			at old dump in charge of the Q.M.S, Cohn. Same day decided to move dump site further from enemy fire & earmarked new dump site at A 2 a 1.5. H.Q. moved at 10.30 am to camp at A 2 d 66. All other section moved to new camping grounds i.e. A1d + A2c. Rained continually & grounds was very soft. Received reports that Reinf. Men at A4 & loads not handed for FRICOURT. Some time ago B Echelon reported was moved to move back to FRICOURT. Owing to the excessive blocking on the roads, the waggons did not return to camp until very late. OC OT & Section decided to move early next morning.	
	21st		A Schelon moved back & camp at F + d. Ammunition train arrived at OLD FRICOURT Station during the night & Lorries no longer able to bring up Ammunition. In 4 section pay more than very expected.	
	20th		All sections of A Schelon got loads shells & but carried waggon there, but only 3 men of Schel tin were killed outright. A lot of equipment - officer mess gear were blown up including No 1 section mens cart + tent.	
	22		A Schelon helped to cart Ammunition from next advances dumps.	

Army Form C. 2118.

WAR DIARY
or
INTELLIGENCE SUMMARY.
(Erase heading not required.)

Place	Date	Hour	Summary of Events and Information	Remarks and references to Appendices
MONTAUBAN.	22d		Weather remained fine the whole of the day & roads are drying up rapidly. Horses only being in hard - expect reinforcement horses tonight. Reinforcement animals did not arrive until late tonight. They were sent immediately to join the Brigade & section. Weather remained fine - Army getting up ammunition.	
	23d		82 Remounts (mules) arrived for 87A. Column have been hyper. 2/Lt S.C. Collins reports his arrival from 33 S.R. Received order to send Bulletting parties to BONNAY on 1st Oct.	
	30			

A W C Bainbridge Colonel
Commanding 14 R.H.A.

Vol 14

Confidential

War Diary

of

14th Divisional Ammunition Column.

From October 1st to October 31st 1916.

Volume XVIII

WAR DIARY or INTELLIGENCE SUMMARY

Army Form C. 2118.

14 S.A.C. R.F.A.

Place	Date	Hour	Summary of Events and Information	Remarks and references to Appendices
MONTAUBAN	1/10/16		Received orders for 14 S.A. to withdraw from 1st Corps Area. Sent Billetting party under 2/Lt Lucie Smith to BONNAY to arrange for Billets. Handed over the Adv. Ammunition Dump to 21st S.A.C.	
	2/10/16		Marched to Billets at BONNAY – weather very wet. Arrived at BONNAY at about 5 p.m. Very few billets available – men mostly slept under wagon covers.	
	3/10/16		Continued march to MOLLIENS with 4/5: Adv. + Train Sections.	
	4"		Marched to billets in AUTHIEULE	
	5		Marched to billets in LATTRE ST QUENTIN. 33rd S.A.C. had just moved out & consequently the billets were very crowded. Sent L. 21 Ammn Section Sergeant	
	6"		Sent Lt LLEWELLIN to take over Adv. Dump from 12 S.A.C. at SIEMENCOURT. Capt McCulloch posted to A/47 and ceased to join Lt LLEWELLIN appointed Town Commandant at SIEMENCOURT	
	7"		Marched to billets at FOSSEUX. Capt Hawkins Smith took over duties of Town Major at Sorieux.	
	8"		No 3 sub. marched from Lattre St QUENTIN to billets at SIEMENCOURT the Ordnance Section and took over the Adv. Dump.	

WAR DIARY
or
INTELLIGENCE SUMMARY

Army Form C. 2118.

14 D.A.C. RFA.

Place	Date	Hour	Summary of Events and Information	Remarks and references to Appendices
	October 1916			
	22"		Lt. Hughes attaches to No. 3 Sect. and is appointed O.C. Dump. Received 4 G.S. waggons (complete turnouts) from 528 Howitzer Battery + posts to B. Ech.: also 4 complete turnouts 4.5 Ammunition waggons and pints to A Column.	
	23"		2/Lt O'Brien attaches to No 3 Sect from No 2 Section. A.D.V.S. VI Corps inspects all animals of D.A.C.	
	24"		The S.O.C. presented Military Medals (ribbons) to Q.M.S. Lee of No 2 Sect and Sgt Baily, Sgr Pearce, while Trumpeter, L/C Rednick all of No 1 Sect.	
	26		6.42 Inf Brigade arrived at FOSSEUX on their way out – being relieved by 36 Inf Bde (12" Div). Since arrival at FOSSEUX and SIEMENCOURT, the Column has been mainly occupied in building winter quarters – particulars Stable and Standings for horses.	
	31		G.O.C. RA VI Corps visited the camp & paid particular attention to Horse Lines & stables.	

CurrBrock Lt Colonel

CONFIDENTIAL.

WAR DIARY

OF

14TH DIVISIONAL AMMUNITION COLUMN

From 1st November 1916.   To 30th November 1916

(Volume ~~XIX~~)

WAR DIARY
or
INTELLIGENCE SUMMARY. 14 D.A.C — R.F.A

Army Form C. 2118.

(Erase heading not required.)

Place	Date	Hour	Summary of Events and Information	Remarks and references to Appendices
FOSSEUX	Nov 1/16	9:0"	Capt Lewis R.A.M.C. proceeds on leave. Vice relieved by Capt Booth. Senior N.C.O's attend lecture on the new smoke box respirator at BERNEVILLE.	
	16		C.R.A. visits Pa. Lewitts & Lim. of No 3 Sect (aug). 19 Reinforcements arrived.	
	17			
	18		Set up a vanish entrenchment for the men of the Sec.	
	20"		No 1 Sect relieves No III section as adv section at SIEMENCOURT	
	21		G.O.C. 14 Divis visited the Column ranfette and horse standings & billetts both at Siemencourt & FOSSEUX.	

Awdbrech Lt Colonel
Comdg 14 DAC

WAR DIARY

of

14TH DIVISIONAL AMMUNITION COLUMN

From 1st December 1916.   To, 31st December 1916.

(Volume XX)

WAR DIARY
or
INTELLIGENCE SUMMARY. 14 D.A.C. R.F.A

Army Form C. 2118.

(Erase heading not required.)

Instructions regarding War Diaries and Intelligence Summaries are contained in F.S. Regs., Part II. and the Staff Manual respectively. Title pages will be prepared in manuscript.

Place	Date	Hour	Summary of Events and Information	Remarks and references to Appendices
FOSSEUX	December 1916			
	3rd		Drew up ammunition from Park & compete war section.	
		6²	2/Lt Taylor & Belletty proc. Staff car bellett at IVERGNY	
	7		Marches to IVERGNY starting at abt 10am. Adv: Section started 6 p.m. after landing over to 12: D.A.C.	
	10th		G.O.C R.A. Inspects the D.A.C. (with the exception of no 3 section) in div. reserve ammunition	
	14th		2/Lt A.S.H. O'Brien left to join the R.F.C at HESDIN	
	15		The Adjudant takes on auto. of T. Major, IVERGNY.	
	18		G.o.C R.A. inspects No 3 Sect in Div. reserve (ammunition)	
	23rd		2/Lt O'Brien A.S.H. & El Sgt Francis B.O. evacuated (on R.A.R.O 933 at 23rd inst.)	

Auversmith
Lt Col
Amy 14 DAC

C O N F I D E N T I A L

W A R   D I A R Y

of

14th Divisional Ammunition Column.

From - January 1st. 1917.   To - January 31st, 1917.

Volume 21.

WAR DIARY

Army Form C. 2118.

INTELLIGENCE SUMMARY. 14 D.A.C - R.F.A

Place	Date	Hour	Summary of Events and Information	Remarks and references to Appendices
IVERGNY	2/1/17		Received orders reorganising the Column viz. No 3 Sect thrown + & A F A B C No 1 + 2 Section are the slightly increased strength and 13 batteries the new	
		4ᵗʰ	The new organization put into effect by transferring 7 G.S. wagons viz limbers + drivers from 13 batteries to No 1 + 2 section + 4, 18ᵖʳ limbers + 4, 4.5 limbers to S.A.A limbers wagons from + drivers from No 3 Section	
		2ⁿᵈ	Review after operation order No. 69 to Marnel & JOSSEUX & SIEMENCOURT batteries the 12 D.A.C as him -	
		3ʳᵈ	Received & manage conversation	
		5ᵗʰ	Received 1 water cart from 46 + the 20 sniphin mieting bores + 2/Lt E de PIERRES	
		6ᵗʰ	Received orders amending the date of 0.0.69 bored 7" 6" 4.5" inches 3" 4" 13" 2/Lt de PIERRE'S pants to No 4 sect rec 2/Lt CLIFTON + from No. 4 section parts to No. 1 section. 2/Lt HOLFORD WALKER joined from No. 9; Driver + parts to No. III section	
		7ᵗʰ	2/Lt E V GOODMAN, 2/Lt W.E. FLETCHER, 2/Lt N.T. McCLAKE joined from base + parties sections 2, H.B.A.Tan Battalion respectively	
		8	0.0.69 came into effect. No 1 Section proceeded to SIEMENCOURT	

WAR DIARY
or
INTELLIGENCE SUMMARY. 14 DAC RFA

Army Form C. 2118.

Place	Date	Hour	Summary of Events and Information	Remarks and references to Appendices
GOUY	8"		an advanced section, H.Q. forming no nexus to FOSSEUX, provides to GOUY - H.Q. Offrs & nearly 3 of . Sectn II. 48 A.C + B Sector, remove hurned am ammunition B12 SAC. Horses are built to FOSSEUX have but taken on by VII Corps Camp + Waggon lines taken on from 12 SAC am is very dirty + wanting condition. Capt A. MACKLOW SMITH Renders and T.M. IVERGNY to Capt Sr. LORIMER of 5" Cameron Highlanders. Capt LLEWELLIN becomes duties of T.M. FOSSEUX and 2/Lt CLIFTON appointed T.M. SIEMENCOURT.	
	9"		2/Lt. W BROWN joins from 35" Div. Sparks 8 ho / Sect.	
	14		19 S Waggon 2, 4 S Amb Waggon + 6.15 p am. Waggon arrives from H.T. Depot, ABBEVILLE Acomplete H & A F.A - BAC	
	15		H & A F A - BAC came under 48 Bde for administration but remain attached to 14 SAC for discipline and tactical purposes.	
	26"		48 Bde moves from FOSSEUX to GOUY and occupies beleth hime.	
	31"		H.Q. ovens to him from GOUY to BARLY track room for 30 SAC coming into GOUY	

AArchibald Lt RA

CONFIDENTIAL.

WAR DIARY.

OF

14th DIVISIONAL AMMUNITION COLUMN.

From 1st February, 1917 to 28th February, 1917.

Volume 22.

WAR DIARY
INTELLIGENCE SUMMARY

14 DAC - RFA

Army Form C. 2118.

Place	Date	Hour	Summary of Events and Information	Remarks and references to Appendices
BARLY	1917			
	3rd Feb		Capt Gwin RAMC returns to report to 43 Div: Ambulance. Lt Gibson RAMC joins vice 'Gwin' posted to England. B/Genuine Landry temporary takes up	
	4"		Leaving for 19th Corps. Lt Gibson RAMC returns & attends Sanitary Course at St Pol. Relieved by Capt W. Macleod who joined same day. Lt Gibson admitted to No 12 Stationary Hospital	
	14		2/Lt G.H. Scott joined from No 2 Base with 19 other ranks. Pte Scott Ptes Khoi Sect.	
	18		all traffic suspended until 21st inst on account of the state of the snow covered by the thaws. 2/Lt Moore takes over V Corps Ammn dump at GOUY	
	21st		Thaw continued until 24th inst	
	22-26		nothing unusual to report	
	27		Lt GOC. RA visits Lun line artillery HQ. No 2 sec'd of Wickham at POZEUX	

AncBurnett
Lt Col
Cmng 14 DAC

[3 MAR 1917 stamp: HQrs 14th Div Ammunition Column]

CONFIDENTIAL.

WAR DIARY

OF

14th Divisional Ammunition Column.

From 1st March, 1917 to - 31st March, 1917.

Volume 23.

Army Form C. 2118.

WAR DIARY
or
INTELLIGENCE SUMMARY.
(Erase heading not required.)

14TH D.A.C. — R.F.A.

Instructions regarding War Diaries and Intelligence Summaries are contained in F. S. Regs., Part II. and the Staff Manual respectively. Title pages will be prepared in manuscript.

Place	Date	Hour	Summary of Events and Information	Remarks and references to Appendices
BARLY	1919 MARCH. 10		Rev. F.C. Downman is attached to Ad Clos w/r from 1.3.19. The undermentioned Offrs proceeded from the Column to Batteries for one months instruction: 2nd Lieut E.V. Grootham No 2 Sec. to 47th Bde and 2nd Lieut M.T.M. Clarke 7 B Echelon to 46th Bde. The undermentioned Offrs was attached to the Column Lieut S. Milner 7 46th Bde to B Echelon 2nd Lieut G Crompton 7 47th Bde to No 2. 2nd Lieut G.H. Scott 7 No 1. attached to 3rd Army Medium Trench Mortar School	
	13		In a convoy of ambulances Captain H.R. Pennington, R.A.M.C. Army reported to 43rd Field Ambulance & Clos vice Capt. MacLeod is attached to During the earlier part of the month the Column had been transporting Rations, Forage from Railhead at Sandley to Refill Point at Gouy, Toby V.G, When was struck by an Influenza our ammunition supply work and began the nightly ammunition from Corps Dump at Railway Bridge Demicourt to the Batteries.	
	18		The B.O.C. 14th Div and C.R.A. 14th Div inspected the horses of the column 2nd Lieut E.V. Grootham of No 2 Section in posted to 46th Bde R.F.A.	

WAR DIARY or INTELLIGENCE SUMMARY.

Army Form C. 2118.

14th D.A.C. — R.F.A.

Place	Date	Hour	Summary of Events and Information	Remarks and references to Appendices
BARLY	1917 MARCH. 19		Lieut. G. Hilmer of B/46th Bde is posted to No Column w.e.f 15.3.17.	
	21		2nd Lieut. S.H. Scott rejoins No 1 Section from 3rd Army T.M. School. 2nd Capt. S.H. Phillips & Lieut H.B. Davis are posted to the D.A.C.	
SIMENCOURT	23		Hd Qrs 14th D.A.C. and No II & III Sections 14th D.A.C. vacated their billets at BARLY and FOSSEUX respectively and moved into SIMENCOURT. when they were billeted as follows. Hd Qrs office - Hut at No 8 HIGH STREET. Horse Lines No 24 HIGH STREET. No II & III Sections Men Billets in 8 Nissen Huts left of SIMENCOURT - BERNEVILLE Rd at Q 11. a 5.9. Horse lines - on opposite side of road in an open field at Q 11 a 6.4. (Sheet 51C 1/20,000) 20 wagons for A.S.C. supplies and 10 for R.E. material was the daily fatigue at this time, while in addition ammunition was carried for the Divnl SIMENCOURT to the 48th Bde Batteries. 2nd Lieut R. Brown rejoins No 1 Section from the 4007 Army Dump. Lieut A.B. Davis is posted to 47 Bde R.Q.M. w.e.f 22/3/17.	
	26		Captain. R.W. Young having joined the Column from the Base is attached to the Hd Qrs.	

WAR DIARY
or
INTELLIGENCE SUMMARY. 14TH D.A.C. — R.F.A.

Army Form C. 2118.

(Erase heading not required.)

Place	Date	Hour	Summary of Events and Information	Remarks and references to Appendices
SIMENCOURT	MARCH 25. 1917.		Captain Rhodes and party left for BOULOGNE today. They go to bring back 100 remounts by train.	
	30		Captain Alexander O.C. No II Section Army Reserve a special leave proceeded to BELFAST. Captain W.R. Young assumes command during his absence.	
	31		A court of inquiry assembled at Hd. Qrs. today to inquire into and report on the loss of a G.S. wagon belonging to No I Section. This wagon was stolen from the road to the north of SIMENCOURT on the night 25/26 inst. Captain Rhodes returned at 4 p.m. with 99 remounts. These were distributed as follows: 46th Bde 45, 47th Bde 13, D.A.C. 9.	

In the Field
1-4-17

[signature]

Confidential

War Diary

for

D. A. C. (14th.)

1st April to 30th 1917

Volume 24

WAR DIARY
or
INTELLIGENCE SUMMARY. 14TH D.A.C. — R.F.A.

Army Form C. 2118.

(Erase heading not required.)

Place	Date	Hour	Summary of Events and Information	Remarks and references to Appendices
SIMENCOURT.	APRIL 4TH 1917.		CAPT. H.R. RAMSBOTHAM, R.A.M.C. left to join 43rd Field Ambulance. LIEUT. H.F. STEPHENS R.A.M.C. is attached to Hd. Qrs. vice Capt. H.R. RAMSBOTHAM.	
	12TH		2 LIEUT. G. CROMPTON of 47TH Bde is posted to No II Section. Very severe weather was experienced during the first half of the month, snow fell frequently & scarcely a day passed without rain falling. The roads became very heavy with so much traffic & the horse lines in the open had to be shifted from place to place. Stabling in the village was vacated by 37TH D.A.C., A/46 Bde and 26TH M.V.S., II & III Sections when moved into them Jan 48TH B.H.C. — A.F.A. and all the animals were under cover during the last half of the month.	
	15TH		On the night of 12/13 14TH Div. Infantry was relieved by 50TH Div. and 14TH DIV. ARTY. was attached to 50TH DIV. ARTY.	
	16TH		CAPT. ALEXANDER of No II S. section returned from leave and reassumed command of No II Section, acting under orders of C.R.A. 14TH D.W. The following strengths of animals took place. From 14TH D.A.C. 110 L.D. Horses to 46TH Bde. " " " 85 " " " 47TH Bde. The sections contributed as follows No I 45 to 47TH Bde. No. II 60 to 46TH Bde. No. III 50 to 46TH Bde. 10 " 47TH Bde.	

WAR DIARY
or
INTELLIGENCE SUMMARY. 14TH D.A.C. — R.F.A.

Army Form C. 2118.

Place	Date	Hour	Summary of Events and Information	Remarks and references to Appendices
SIMENCOURT	APRIL 1917.			
	16TH		Three animals were inspected by O.C. 14TH D.A.C. and V.O. 14TH D.A.C. before disposition.	
			From 47TH Bde. 20. L.D. horses to 14TH D.A.C.	
			46TH Bde. 13. " " " " " Three animals were posted to	
			No III Section, they were in poor condition and 24 were evacuated.	
			2/Lieut. R.H. STANLEY-WELCH O/C. Amm. Dump SIMENCOURT handed over the dump to Capt. W.R. YOUNG.	
			An Advanced section was formed at DAINVILLE by No I Sec. 14TH D.A.C. when moved up their 18 pdr & 4.5 How Amm. wagons. 2/Lieut DYKE remained at SIMENCOURT	
			i/c S.A.A. section, with animals etc.	
	17TH		Lieut. H.T. MILES is posted to this Column from the horse to taken in the strength.	
			w/e from. 10.4.17 is posted to No I. section and attached to 48TH H.T.A.D. B.A.C.	
	18TH		2/Lieut. R. CLIFTON of No I Section is appointed O.C. Div. Baths & Laundries is attached to Div. Hd. Qrs.	
	19TH		3 Riding horses arrived from the Rear hear through by road, and was taken on strength	No III and 2 posted to Bdes.
	22ND		The advanced section (No I Sec.) moved from DAINVILLE to G 33 d 1.0. Sheet 51 B.1/40000	

Army Form C. 2118.

WAR DIARY
or
INTELLIGENCE SUMMARY. 14TH D.A.C. — R.F.A.
(Erase heading not required.)

Place	Date	Hour	Summary of Events and Information	Remarks and references to Appendices
SIMENCOURT	APRIL 1917			
	22ND.		B.G.-E. HARDING-NEWMAN. C.R.A. 14TH DIV. visited the Column and inspected the animals. At this time in april & jun weather set in, roads & horse lines dried up. 15 ration commencers adopted the arrangement, cleaning and painting of the wagons.	
	27TH		On the night of 26/27 14TH DIV Inf relieved 50TH DIV and 14TH DIV. ARTY ceased to be attached to the 50TH DIV. ARTY.	
	28TH		2/LIEUT BROWN & No I Section took over amm dump at M.18 central (sheet 51B 1/40,000)	
	30TH		10 men from the Column were detailed to assist in the working of the dump. Warm sunny weather still continues, everyone is in chg t the roads dusty. Sick wastage for the month off. 1. O.R. 14.	

In the Field
1/5/17.

A.W.Birch Lt Col
Cmd 14 D.A.C.

C O N F I D E N T I A L.

W A R   D I A R Y.

O F.

14TH DIVISIONAL AMMUNITION COLUMN.

Volume 25.

WAR DIARY or INTELLIGENCE SUMMARY.

Army Form C. 2118.

14TH D.A.C. R.F.A.

Place	Date	Hour	Summary of Events and Information	Remarks and references to Appendices
SIMENCOURT.	MAY-1917			
	1st		The M.O i/c 14TH D.A.C. in conjunction with Town Major SIMENCOURT arranged the following actions for the cleaning & manure from the farmyards in the commune. II & III Sections each furnished 4 teams daily, these were horsed with farmers wagons and working parties were provided by the infantry. The Wellité in the village. The manure was dumped on the canal and up to the 19th inst when the scheme	
	5TH		Capt. SIMENCOURT much improved with use since (1) in improving the sanitary conditions of the village (11) in assisting the farmers with the cultivation of the land. The installation of BATHS at SIMENCOURT was effected & every man in the column had a bath once a week at this time.	
	10TH		6 L.D. horses and 44 mules of III Section were handed over the 46TH Bde R.F.A. Mules were inspected by M.C.O. and V.O. before departure.	
	11TH		Lieut. H.F. MILLS having rejoined the column was to be attached to 48TH B.A.C. R.F.A. and is posted to No 1 Sect. The following moves took place today	
	14TH		HdQrs 14TH D.A.C. from SIMENCOURT to AGNY Office - PIERRE DE SERBIE Sheet Horses & wagon lines - M.8.d.16 (51c 1/40,000).	

Army Form C. 2118.

WAR DIARY
or
INTELLIGENCE SUMMARY.   14TH D.A.C. — R.F.A.
(Erase heading not required.)

Place	Date	Hour	Summary of Events and Information	Remarks and references to Appendices
ASNY	May 1914			
	19TH		No II Section from SIMENCOURT to ASNY – Horse & Wagon Lines at M.8.c 6.5.	
			No III " " " " " " " " " M.8a 7.6.	
			No I Sect detached from SIMENCOURT to rejoin I Section at M.18.c 4.5.	
			As rain is three journeys were necessary to effect the move owing to Section being short of animals, then heavy rain hindered us to the Bakrs.	
	20TH		2 Lt. E. LAMB 2/14 T.M.B. is posted to 14TH D.A.C. and further posted to III Sec	
			Fine sunny warm weather was experienced whilst riding then heavy rain fell. S. was the amount at ASNY animals been then not greatly disturbed.	
			They are being their coats and their animals are picking up wonderfully.	
			The G.O.C. and C.R.A. 14TH DIV inspected the Horses at ASNY.	
	23rd.		A party was sent to HURISNY to get remounts. There was 59 in number	
			and in very good condition. The program posted as follows.	
			10 L.D. Horses} No I Sec. 18 L.D. Horses} No II Sec. 4 L.D. Horses} No III Sec.	
			8 mules } 2 mules } 14 mules	
			1 Riding Hd Qtrs. 1 Riding 4. 6TH Bde. 1 Riding 4. 7TH Bde.	
			Weekly training programme was drawn up and 8 saddles starting Munday	

Army Form C. 2118.

WAR DIARY
or
INTELLIGENCE SUMMARY.   14TH D.A.C. — R.F.A.

(Erase heading not required.)

Instructions regarding War Diaries and Intelligence Summaries are contained in F.S. Regs., Part II. and the Staff Manual respectively. Title pages will be prepared in manuscript.

Place	Date	Hour	Summary of Events and Information	Remarks and references to Appendices
ASNY	MAY 1917.			
	23		Training - sig. Marching, rifle, Driving and Riding drills - Lectures in Horse and Stable management - F.A.T. etc. etc. Anthr 2 Lewis Guns a regularly actual was commenced - also consisted of 18 guns 6 gun section. Instruction was given in Semaphore, Morse, Buzzer etc.	
	23		CAPT H.C. ASHENDEN from BASE posted to 14TH D.A.C. and attached to 47nd Bde R.F.A. for duty. 2/LIEUT. N.T.M. CLARKE of No III SEC posted to 46 Bde R.F.A. The A.D.M.S 14TH DIV. visited the Column at ASNY - He inspected the sanitary arrangements, cookhouses etc of Headqtrs, No II, No III Sections.	
	31		With weekly arrangements for month Officers - nil - Other Ranks 11.	

In the Field
1/6/17.

AMcBirnet Lt. Col.
Commdg 14TH D.A.C.

WAR DIARY or INTELLIGENCE SUMMARY

Army Form C. 2118.

14TH D.A.C. R.F.A. Vol 22

Place	Date	Hour	Summary of Events and Information	Remarks and references to Appendices
AGNY.	JUNE 1917.			
	2.		Acting under instructions from Q. 14th Div. areas were allotted to sections for salvage. Military equipment and material was taken to Salvage Dump while agricultural implements while Dud shells were located and marked with a white flag — Men were later collected and blown up by 2.Lt. STANLEY WELCH of No 1 Sec.	
			Lt HUGHES & 2.Lt DE PIERRES left today with a party of men to proceed to ABBEVILLE to collect 280 remounts.	
	3.		2.Lt P.J. LAMB of No III Sec is attached to 14TH DIV. SIGNAL COY for duty.	
	4.		2.Lt COLLINS of No III proceeded on 10 days leave to U.K.	
	5.		Lt HUGHES and party arrived with 200 remounts having journeyed from ABEVILLE by road – 131 L.D. horses were posted to this column as under:–	
			44 L.D. Horses to No I SEC	
			42 " " " No II "	
			44 " " " No III " and 1 L.D. Horse (remount) to 26TH M.V.S.	
	3.		Capt. B.O. MARCH M.C. having joined the division is posted to this Column & is attached to 46TH Bde for duty.	

Army Form C. 2118.

WAR DIARY
or
INTELLIGENCE SUMMARY. 14TH D.A.C
R.F.A.

(Erase heading not required.)

Place	Date	Hour	Summary of Events and Information	Remarks and references to Appendices
AGNY	June 1917			
	5		2 LT. R. CLIFTON of No I SEC having died of wounds is struck off the strength (Army London Gazette dt 5/6/17.) 2 LT CLIFTON was wounded whilst performing in duties of DIV. BATHS. OFFICER when he was detached from his unit. No I SEC. held SUSTN 15 parts — There was a great success altho' showing want of experience.	
	7 + 8		C.R.A. 16TH DIV. took over command of 14TH D.A.	
	10		2 LT DE PIERRES of No III SEC proceeded on 10 days leave to U.K.	
	18		14TH D.A. was relieved by 50TH D.A. The H.R.P at M.15 control was taken over by 50 D.A. 2 LT BROWN O.C. A.R.P. rejoined No I SEC and personnel of regimental section.	
	21		Capt. W. R. YOUNG proceeded on 10 days leave to U.K.	
	24		Capt R.H. RHODES proceeded to SAULTY with party of men to collect 117 remounts. These were posted as follows.—	
			2 L.D. Horses to H.Q. 1 R. Horse to No I. 2 R. Horses to No II.	
			13 L.D. " 30 L.D. "	
			19 L.D. Mules 7 Mules	

WAR DIARY
or
INTELLIGENCE SUMMARY.
(Erase heading not required.)

Army Form C. 2118.

Place	Date	Hour	Summary of Events and Information	Remarks and references to Appendices
AGNY	JUNE 1917 24		1 L.D. Horse	to No III Sec. 10 L.D. to 47th Bde, 34 Mules	
	27		Lt. Taylor + party left HAGNY for ETREE-WAMIN to arrange billets for the Column	
ETREE-WAMIN.	28th		H.Q. No II & III Sections marched from HAGNY at 7.30 a.m. this morning. No I Sec. marched from M.18 Sheet 5113 and proceeded to ETREE-WAMIN via BAC DU NORD, BEAUMETZ and AVESNES arriving by 4 p.m. During the night a violent thunderstorm occurred.	
CROIX	29th		The Column marched from ETREE-WAMIN at 8 a.m. this morning and proceeded to CROIX via BUNEVILLE and RAMECOURT arriving by 1.30 p.m.	
	30		The Column rested today at CROIX — weather showery. Sick Wastage for month 0 — O.R. 14.	

IN THE FIELD.
30. VI. 1917

AWSmith Lt. Col.
Commdg. 14TH D.A.C.

CONFIDENTIAL.

WAR DIARY.

OF.

14TH DIVISIONAL AMMUNITION COLUMN.

From - July 1st, 1917. to July - 31st, 1917.

VOLUME 27.

Army Form C. 2118.

WAR DIARY
or
INTELLIGENCE SUMMARY. 14TH D.A.C. — R.F.A.

(Erase heading not required.)

Instructions regarding War Diaries and Intelligence Summaries are contained in F. S. Regs., Part II. and the Staff Manual respectively. Title pages will be prepared in manuscript.

Place	Date	Hour	Summary of Events and Information	Remarks and references to Appendices
	July 1914.			
NÉDONCHELLE	1st		The column continued the march this morning starting at 5.30 a.m. from CROIX and proceeding via ANVIN, HEUCHIN, and FONTAINE-LES-BOULANS to NEDONCHELLE arriving at 11.30 a.m.	
NEUF PRÉ	2nd		Starting from NEDONCHELLE at 6.30 a.m. the Column proceeded to NEUFPRE and ST MARTIN (AIRE) via NEDON, AMES, ST HILAIRE and LAMBRES. The Column arrived by 10.30 — H.Q. No I & II Section at NEUFPRE No III Sect & Trench Mortars at ST MARTIN.	
ROUGE-CROIX	3RD		The Column marched from NEUFPRE & ST MARTIN at 6.30 this morning and proceeded to ROUGE-CROIX in STRAZEELE — CAESTRE via STEEN BECQUE, MORBECQUE, HAZEBROUCK, BORRÉ and PRADELLES arriving by 11.30 a.m.	
BAILLEUL	4TH		The Column marched from ROUGE-CROIX at 4 p.m. this afternoon & proceeded to camp in sat area 16 m left of METEREN- BAILLEUL Road about 2 kilometres west of BAILLEUL via MOOLENACKER and METEREN arriving by 6. p.m.	
	5TH		The Column halted for one day.	

Army Form C. 2118.

WAR DIARY
or
INTELLIGENCE SUMMARY. 14TH D.A.C.

R.7.4

(Erase heading not required.)

Instructions regarding War Diaries and Intelligence Summaries are contained in F. S. Regs., Part II. and the Staff Manual respectively. Title pages will be prepared in manuscript.

Place	Date	Hour	Summary of Events and Information	Remarks and references to Appendices
	July		1917	
DRANOUTRE	5TH		Billets at DRANOUTRE was taken over from 367TH D.A.C. Capt. G.H. RHODES II Section and personnel for I & II tor ww LINDENHOOK DUMP from 367TH D.A.C.	
	6TH	6.A.M.	The column marched from BAILLEUL to DRANOUTRE relieving 367TH D.A.C. at 6 a.m. The following is the location at - DRANOUTRE - H.Q. Niv No 3 BILLET Horse lines Rebout No 3 Billet No I Section GRAHAMSTOWN Lines No II " NORBURY " No III " DURBAN "	
"	11TH		At 8 a.m. the 37' D.T.C. relieves the 14 S.T.C. but at 9.18 pm 6.H. 5'a.m. waggon 2 G.S. waggon (f/16pr) & 6 G.S. waggon (f. 4.5) with corresponding personnel remained attached to 37 S.T.C. for return. These columns were ordered to commence their detachment. No 2 Section from the S.A.A. section, were attached to 47 S.A. and marched to encamp at N2 d 7 4 (40,000 Belgium sheet 28)	

WAR DIARY
or
INTELLIGENCE SUMMARY. 14TH D.A.C. — R.F.A.

Army Form C. 2118.

Place	Date	Hour	Summary of Events and Information	Remarks and references to Appendices
Near BAILLEUL	July 1917 11th		The remainder of the D.A.C. moves to camp between BAILLEUL & METEREN	
	16th		A Belgian interpreter J.O.S. Van Esch having reported for duty is attached to No III Sec.	
	7th		2/Lieut. V.B. CHRISTIE having joined this division is posted to 14TH D.AC. No III Sec.	
	11th		4/6 June 29/6/17. and 2/Lt DYKE granted 10 days leave to U.K.	
	15th		Lieut HOLMES & 2/Lt DYKE granted 10 days leave to U.K.	
	19th		2/Lt CAMPBELL-ORDE granted 10 days leave to U.K.	
	22nd		2/Lt WELSH - granted 10 days leave to U.K.	
	23rd		LT-COL. A.H.C. BIRCH proceeded on 10 days leave to PARIS.	
	25th		Capt RHODES proceeded on 10 days leave to U.K.	
			D.A.D.V.S. & A.D.V.S. visited the column & inspected Horse lines of No I & III Sec.	
	29th		2/Lt BROWN proceeded on 10 days leave to U.K.	
			LIEUT. MILLS No I Sec. attached to 41st A.R.P. for duty	
	26th		CAPT. B.O. MARCH having transferred to 31st D.A. is struck off strength of us	

Army Form C. 2118.

WAR DIARY
or
INTELLIGENCE SUMMARY. 14TH D.A.C. — R.F.A.

(Erase heading not required.)

Instructions regarding War Diaries and Intelligence Summaries are contained in F. S. Regs., Part II. and the Staff Manual respectively. Title pages will be prepared in manuscript.

Place	Date	Hour	Summary of Events and Information	Remarks and references to Appendices
BAILLEUL	July 1917 29th			
	30TH		Snow Manoeuvres occurred today and much rain fell and it seems that the recent spell of hot weather has changed to a spell of wet. O.C. No II Sec. attached 47th D.H. reports casualties from shell fire 2 drivers wounded — 5 drivers wounded — 6 L.D. animals killed whilst proceeding to Battery position with ammunition. Sick wastage for month — Offs - nil. O.R. 1.	
			In the Field. 2/VIII/17.	

WCBird Lt.Col.
Commdg. 14TH D.A.C.

Vol 24

War Diary for

14th Divisional Ammunition Column

for

August – 1917.

H.Q., R.A.
14th DIVISION
No............
Date............

Volume 28.

WAR DIARY
INTELLIGENCE SUMMARY

Army Form C. 2118.

14TH D.A.C. – R.7.A

Place	Date	Hour	Summary of Events and Information	Remarks and references to Appendices
BAILLEUL	AUGUST 1917.			
	4.		2/Lt. B.H. Scott proceeded on 10 days leave to U.K.	
	6.		Capt. A. Macklow-Smith & 2/Lt. G. Crompton proceeded on 10 days leave to U.K. No III Sec. (advanced section attached to 41st DA) came out of action & moved camp from N 2 d 8.9 to M 16 b 9.5 Shot 28 '40,000.	
	8.		2Lt. E.N. de Pierres } No III Sec. is transferred to 41st D.A.	
	9.		2Lt. S.C. Collins with details from No I & III Sec. under his command came to be attached to 37th D.A.C. at DRANOUTRE & rejoins his own section.	
	10.		Brig. Gen. E. Harding-Newman – C.R.A. 14th Div. visited the D.A.C. today & inspected the horses of H.Q. No I & III Secs. Capt. N. Macphail R.A.M.C. reported this morning & is attached temporarily as M.O. of 14th DAC, whilst Lt. Stephens R.A.M.C. is on leave Lt. Stephens R.A.M.C. proceeded on 10 days leave to U.K.	
	11		No 710516 Dr Gorse.T. of No II Section awarded the Military Medal for act of gallantry in the field.	
	10		About 9.30 this morning a 9" shell from a long range gun landed in the	

WAR DIARY
~~INTELLIGENCE SUMMARY~~. 14TH D.A.C. — R.F.A.

Army Form C. 2118.

(Erase heading not required.)

Place	Date	Hour	Summary of Events and Information	Remarks and references to Appendices
BAILLEUL	AUGUST 1917.			
	10		Camp of "B" Echelon unmaking 2 Lt. V.G. Christie and 4 other ranks whilst 2.O.R. were killed. 9 mules were killed and several wounded.	
OUDERDOM	11		At 11.30 a.m. the column marched from BAILLEUL to OUDERDOM 28 O 29 d 9.9. via ST JANS CAPPEL, WESTOUTRE and RENINGHELST arriving at 2.30 p.m.	
			The 14th D.A. is now in II CORPS and attached to 18TH D.A.	
	12TH		Ammunition supply started at once - refilling at CORDOVA dump and delivering to battery position S + S.E. of ZILLEBEKE.	
			Rain fell heavily making roads very heavy - especially near battery positions when it is almost impossible to get wagons through. New ammn. will arrive.	
	16TH		Lt. H.J.M ??? of No I Sec. proceeded on 10 days leave to U.K.	
	18TH		2/Lt. CAMPBELL-ORDE and 2.O.R. wounded whilst delivering ammn to guns.	
	19TH		Lt. H.J. MILLS of No I Sec. is transferred to 47TH D.A.C. R.F.A.	
			CAPT. S.J. ALEXANDER of No II Sec. proceeded on 10 days leave to U.K.	
	22ND		2/Lt. R. BROWN of No I Sec. is attached to CORDOVA Dump for duty.	
			CAPT. MACPHAIL left to join 42ND F.A. and ceases to be attached to this unit.	

Army Form C. 2118.

WAR DIARY
or
INTELLIGENCE SUMMARY. 14TH D.A.C. – R.F.A

(Erase heading not required.)

Instructions regarding War Diaries and Intelligence Summaries are contained in F. S. Regs., Part II. and the Staff Manual respectively. Title pages will be prepared in manuscript.

Place	Date	Hour	Summary of Events and Information	Remarks and references to Appendices
OUDERDOM	AUGUST 1917.			
	22		2/Lt S.C. COLLINS 1 B Battn Army Rem cemented sick is struck off the strength	
	26		A draft of 80 reinforcements arrived Rem today – 8 drivers of this group was posted to 14TH D.A.C. the remainder to Batteries.	
	27		2/Lt (STANLEY) WELCH proceeded to PROVEN to collect 80 L.D remounts. T/hese were posted as follows. 46TH Bde. 20 47TH Bde. 30. 14TH D.H.C. 30 Seven Mark stores & goods were expressed – ammunition empty still continues It is impossible to get new wagons to our Batteries but specks Rem her Brown to facilitate relieving	
	29		24 L.D. remounts were collected from PROVEN today and distributed as follows 47TH Bde 5. 14TH D.H.C. 19. No 60235 Cpl. COOKSEY W. and No 65668. Dr MURPHY J. both of B Echelon 14TH D.A.C. were awarded the Military Medal for Gallantry in the field.	

1577 Wt.W.10791/1773 500,000 1/15 D. D. & L.   A.D.S.S./Forms/C. 2118.

WAR DIARY or **INTELLIGENCE SUMMARY.** 14th D.A.C. — R.F.A.

Army Form C. 2118.

Place	Date	Hour	Summary of Events and Information	Remarks and references to Appendices
OUDERDOM	August 1917 31st		The following is a list of casualties for the month. Killed Wounded Evacuated Personnel 6 O.R. 29. 8 O.R. 19. 8 O.R. Animals 23 23 and 2 18 pdr. amm. wagons were destroyed by shell fire. In the Field. 1/IX/17	Aurebuch Lt. Col. Commdg. 14th D.A.C.

WAR DIARY

FOR

14TH DIVISIONAL AMMUNITION COLUMN RFA

FOR

SEPTEMBER 1917.

WAR DIARY
or
INTELLIGENCE SUMMARY. 14TH D.A.C. — R.F.A.
(Erase heading not required.)

Army Form C. 2118.

Place	Date	Hour	Summary of Events and Information	Remarks and references to Appendices
OUDERDOM	SEPT. 1917 2nd		No 93572 A/Bdr N. LENNIE & No 1 Sec. awarded the Military Medal.	
	3rd		A high explosive bomb was dropped by an enemy aeroplane in the camp of H.Q.s. killing 1 O.R. and wounding 3 O.R. The following awarded Military Medals. 69936 Dvr H. SKIPWORTH No I Sec. 103769 Dvr J.L. CRAIK No III. 59942 " G. ETHERIDGE No I Sec. 98353 " J.A. GIFFORD No II. CAPT. W.R. YOUNG. afterwards 14TH D.A.C. is posted to 47TH Bde R.F.A.	
	5th 6th		14TH D.A. was today transferred from IInd to VIII Corps. The column marched from OUDERDOM at 12.15 p.m. and proceeded to NEUVE-EGLISE area via RENINGHELST,	
NEUVE EGLISE.			WEST OUTRE, LOCRE and DRANOUTRE arriving in camp at 3 p.m. As the 1 Gun and wagons to follow. H.Qrs. 28 T 9 c 4.1. No I Sec 28 T 14 8.6. No II Sec 28 T 9 c 4.7. No III Sec 26 T 8 c 6.3. at present horses & men are milled in the open.	
	7th		A draft of 17 O.R. arrived today.	

Army Form C. 2118.

WAR DIARY
or
INTELLIGENCE SUMMARY. 14TH D.A.C. ——— R.F.A.
(Erase heading not required.)

Instructions regarding War Diaries and Intelligence Summaries are contained in F. S. Regs., Part II. and the Staff Manual respectively. Title pages will be prepared in manuscript.

Place	Date	Hour	Summary of Events and Information	Remarks and references to Appendices
NEUVE EGLISE	Sept. 1917.			
	8TH		LIEUT. HUGHES No II Sec. is appointed VIII Corps Reinhard Officer at O.X.F. Reinhard. He proceeded to DE KENNE BAK for duty.	
	9TH		Ammn Supply 110 guns commenced. 2 drops of 110 OR & 12 OR arrived today. 10 OR arrived today.	
	15TH			
	18TH		The loading of tanks for what was started today. 7 is OR are being drawn for nymph & Concrete Bunkers & Brick for stoveking.	
	24TH		The C.R.A. 14TH D.A. visited the section today.	
	29TH		14TH D.A. visited the section today. A maximum speed of day worth has been experimented this month. This has greatly facilitated the erection of stores.	
	30TH		The following is a list of casualties for the month	
			Killed Wounded accidental airtinjur	
			Personnel OR 1 3 14	
			Animals 2 4	
			In The Field 1/X/17. Cunnsnsh Lt. Col. Comdg. 14TH D. A.C.	

WAR DIARY FOR

OCTOBER - 1917

OF

14TH DIVISIONAL AMMUNITION COLUMN R.F.A.
-----o-----

VOLUME 30.

Volume 30

Original

Army Form C. 2118.

WAR DIARY
or
INTELLIGENCE SUMMARY. 14TH D.A.C. — R.F.A.

(Erase heading not required.)

Instructions regarding War Diaries and Intelligence Summaries are contained in F.S. Regs., Part II. and the Staff Manual respectively. Title pages will be prepared in manuscript.

Place	Date	Hour	Summary of Events and Information	Remarks and references to Appendices
NEUVE EGLISE	OCTOBER 1917. 3		Fine weather still continues. Erection of shelter is proceeding rapidly.	
	4		Heavy rain fell today.	
	5		Capt. J.P.B. EASTWOOD of No I Sec. proceeded in 10 days leave to U.K.	
	7		At 10 a.m. this morning all clocks & watches were put back one hour than country Summer to GREENWICH time.	
	10		Lt. C. STUART & 2Lt. H.J. TUBBS joined this Column from 8TH Div. Arty). They are taken on the strength & posted to No 2 Section.	
	11		Capt. G.H. RHODES i/c 10 O.R. proceeded to BOULOGNE today to draw 20 Remounts & bring back by road. A draft of 8 O.R. arrived here this evening.	
			2Lt. CROMPTON and 5 O.R. proceeded to 4th Army School of Mortars to attend a 13 days course in Medium T.M.s.	
	13.		Lt. W.C.T. aghu proceeded in 10 days leave to U.K.	
			2Lt. N.R. PAKENHAM-WALSH having today joined this column is taken on the strength & posted to No III Section.	

Army Form C. 2118.

WAR DIARY
or
INTELLIGENCE SUMMARY.
(Erase heading not required.)

14TH D.A.C. — R.F.A.

Place	Date	Hour	Summary of Events and Information	Remarks and references to Appendices
NEUVE EGLISE	OCTOBER 1917. 15		2Lt. G.H. Scott having posted to Y/14 T.M.B. is struck off the strength of No I Section.	
	16		2Lts. G.H. Scott & G. Crompton are authorised to wear the badge of the rank of Lieut. pending announcement in LONDON GAZETTE.	
	18		2Lt. W.P. P-Walsh having been posted to 104 A.F.A. Bde. is struck off the strength of No III Section.	
	20		Rev. L.C. Downman having been transferred to Hazebrouck district ceases to be attached to H.Q.	
	30		The erection of stores has proceeded apace during the month. H.Q., I & III Sections have practically completed their standings while II Section is next up for roofing materials, much work having yet to be done in regards etc.	
	31		Casualties for the month. Personnel – O.R. wounded 6. Animals " " 7.	

In The Field. 2/11/17.

auerBuchn
Lt. Col.
Cmdg. 14TH D.A.C.

CONFIDENTIAL.

WAR DIARY

FOR

NOVEMBER = 1917

14TH. DIVISIONAL AMMUNITION COLUMN R.F.A.

Volume XXXI.

Army Form C. 2118.

WAR DIARY
or
INTELLIGENCE SUMMARY. 14TH D.A.C. R.F.A.
(Erase heading not required.)

Instructions regarding War Diaries and Intelligence Summaries are contained in F.S. Regs., Part II. and the Staff Manual respectively. Title pages will be prepared in manuscript.

Place	Date	Hour	Summary of Events and Information	Remarks and references to Appendices
NEUVE EGLISE	Nov. 1917.			
	2.		Capt. H. MACKLOW-SMITH Adjt. 14TH D.A.C. is attached to 14TH R.A. H.Q. for 1 month.	
	4.		Lt. Col. M.H.C. BIRCH Cmdg 14TH D.H.C. having proceeded on 14 days leave to U.K. Capt. S.J. ALEXANDER assumes temporary command.	
	6.		A reinforcement - draft of 157 drivers arrived today - a/15 in speed of drivers wanted, rise ad in to the mouth. Arrears unsettled & etc.	
	5.		Capt. J. PENROSE of III See proceeded on 14 days leave to U.K.	
	11		Lt. H.W.H. DYKE of I See proceeded on 14 days leave to U.K.	
WATOU	18.		The Column marched from NEUVE EGLISE at 8 a.m. this morning and proceeded to WATOU AREA via DRANOUTRE - LOCRE - WESTOUTRE and ABEELE arriving at 2 p.m. There is no cover for MT animals which are standing in open fields. The men are in huts and farms. Location. H.Q. Offices at - TRAPPISTES FARM 27 K 19 A 1.3. Lines 27 K 16 d 9.9	
			No I Section at - 27 K 3 d 5.5	
			No II Section at - 27 K 3 d 9.8	
			No III Section at - 27 K 3 c 4.2	

WAR DIARY
or
INTELLIGENCE SUMMARY.
(Erase heading not required.)

Army Form C. 2118.

Place	Date	Hour	Summary of Events and Information	Remarks and references to Appendices
WATOU	Nov. 1917 20TH		Capt. G.H. RHODES. proceeded on 14 days leave to U.K. Lt. WELSH & 2Lt BROWN of No I S.C. proceeded to PICKERING DUMP at 28 I 2 b 2.5 when they are attached for duty. 14TH R.A.H.Q. opened at 28 I 1d 9.5.	
VLAMERTINGHE	24TH		The column marched this morning at 10 a.m. and proceeded to VLAMERTINGHE via ST JAN DER BIEZEN and SWITCH ROAD. 27 L 5 d 7-5 — 28 G 3 c 9.3. Camps and Lines of 2ND CANADIAN D.A.C. were taken over as follows. H.Q. Office at 28 H 9 d 0.6. Lines at 28 H 9 c 5.5. No I S at 28 H 9 c central. " II " " 28 H 9 c central. " III " " 28 H 9 c central. Men and Officers are billeted in Nissen huts - Animals are in an open field with neither cover or standings. Ammunition supply started today, all amm. is taken up by packs, filling up at PICKERING Dump 28 I 2 b 2.5 or OXFORD DUMP 28 C 28 d 6 2.3, on the way up to the positions at-	
	26TH			

Army Form C. 2118.

WAR DIARY
or
INTELLIGENCE SUMMARY. 14TH D.A.C. — R.F.A.

(Erase heading not required.)

Place	Date	Hour	Summary of Events and Information	Remarks and references to Appendices
VLAMERTINGHE	Nov 1917.			
	26TH		at 28 D/14 & 28 D/15 astride the road.	
			On the way north gun position convoy was shelled - casualties No 1 Sec. 2 O.R. wounded. 2 horses killed & wounded. Amn Supply continues daily - chiefly to D/46 & D/47.	
	29TH		With an Amn dump is in progress — driveways & road making.	
	30TH		On the morning of the 29TH the enemy started shelling VLAMERTINGHE AREA with high velocity shell calibre uncertain 4·2" or 6" Shelly intermittent continued until 5 p.m. 30TH inst. Casualties No IV Sec 2 O.R. wounded.	
			Casualties for the month.	
			Personnel. Evacuated Wounded.	
			10. O.R. 4. O.R.	
			Animals. 2. 2.	

In The Field. 30/XI/17.

Ancisworth Lt.Col.
Cmdg. 14TH D.A.C.

35807. W16879 M1879 500,000 3/17 R.T. (1074) Forms W3091/3   Army Form W.3091.

Cover for Documents.

Nature of Enclosures.

W A R   D I A R I E S

F O R

D E C E M B E R - 1917

1 4 T H . D . A . C . & ~~TRENCH MORTAR BATTERIES.~~

Notes, or Letters written.

WAR DIARY
INTELLIGENCE SUMMARY. 14TH D.A.C.

Army Form C. 2118.

R.7.A.

Place	Date	Hour	Summary of Events and Information	Remarks and references to Appendices
VLAMERTINGHE	Dec. 1914. 3.		Lieut Dyke and party were today detailed to relieve guns from the gun line; a party of 20 men were provided. They went with a G.S. wagon & gun limber. Proceeded to the gun line at 2 p.m. to relieve guns.	
	8.		The D.A.D.V.S. inspected the animals today - he was well satisfied with them.	
	10.		The C.R.A. 14th D.A. today visited the column and inspected materiel. A draft of 10 Drivers R.T.A. & for 14th D.A. current today.	
	11.		3 ofr. 90 O.R. arrived today - requirements for 14th D.A. Orders were received to reorganise the column. This means a reduction in establishment and the conversion of B echelon with an S.A.A. section.	
	13.		No 42 Dr Broom H. No I Sec. 14th D.A.C. awarded M.M. Capt. A. McLellan Smith proceeded on 14 days leave to U.K.	
	14.		The G.O.C. & C.R.A. 14th Div. visited the column this morning & 20 mules fitted with pouches infantry and loaded with Trench Brench's & Barthel win & ammo screw pickets. The men were training mules to carry packs as we are to be an now training mules to carry packs as we are to	

Army Form C. 2118.

WAR DIARY
or
INTELLIGENCE SUMMARY. 14TH D.A.C. — R.F.A.
(Erase heading not required.)

Place	Date	Hour	Summary of Events and Information	Remarks and references to Appendices
	Dec. 1917.			
VLAMERTINGHE	19		Transport R.E. material from R.E. dump Ypres. The arrangements is now completed. 18 wagons G.S. and 1 mule cart have been allotted us to entrainer, also surplus lorries for same. The pulling animals have been allotted us: 40 to 64th Bde. M.F.H. 23 to 46 Bde R.F.A. 21 to 47th Bde R.F.A. and 11 to 14th Div. Tps. Pack animals have been allotment of as follows: 28 O.R. to 64th Bde A.F.A. 12 O.R. to 50th D.A.C. 12 O.R. to 46 Bde R.F.A. 20 O.R. to 47th Bde R.F.A.	
	20.		The entraining of Staffs has proceeded steadily all the animals & the S.A.H. Section & Hdq an now under care of the orderlies & details for No II Sec is proceeding apace.	
	22.		The C.R.A. visited the column this morning. 20 Wms & 30 mules proceed to PACK LINES YPRES. They are to the engaged carrying up R.E. material from BILGE Dump to BELLEVUE.	

WAR DIARY
INTELLIGENCE SUMMARY. 14TH D.A.C.

Army Form C. 2118.

R.7.A

Place	Date	Hour	Summary of Events and Information	Remarks and references to Appendices
VLAMERTINGHE	DEC 1917			
	25		Snow fell today & it is bitterly cold.	
	26		A new clergy arrived as so money as far as finish. Owing to the frosty weather Gun Sections for the present has stopped. Return the 3rd & 22nd 12 guns & a quantity of items have been returned.	
	27		A large amount of steel previously returned has been returned. No II Section has had a waggon sent down daily carrying steel from my warehouse between WILTJE and SOREL FARM. Up to the present about 30000 Rods 18 feet & 4'5" steel, with & 7000 wth of all arms.	
	30		7 horses sick in today, men & part mainly changeover.	
	31		Lt Holmes & Jowett returned for YPRES today. Since the 18th inst. the 14TH D.A.C. has supplied all necessary transport for 126 A.F.A. Bde. This has entailed much extra work. Six Waggons for mule. O.R. 12 minute 10.	

In The Field

ANC Burch Lt. Cn.
Cmdg. 14TH D.A.C.

Army Form C. 2118.

Original

WAR DIARY
or
INTELLIGENCE SUMMARY.   14TH D.A.C.
R.F.A.

(Erase heading not required.)

Place	Date	Hour	Summary of Events and Information	Remarks and references to Appendices
VLAMERTINGHE.	JAN. 1918. 1st		Lts. STUART, LAMB and WELSH and Sibbly Party left VLAMERTINGHE Siding to go on ahead and biller for the Column.	
OUDEZEELE.	2nd	8.30 a.m.	The Column marched from Vlamertinghe and proceeded via POPERINGHE and WATOU to OUDEZEELE arriving there at 2.30 p.m. and going into billets at VLAMERTINGHE was handed over to 8TH D.A.C. Camps, Area Stores etc being carried with arms & kit. The roads were in a bad state.	
RENESCURE.	3rd		Last night there was a heavy fall of snow and this morning the roads were in a still worse condition. The D.A.C. was due to march at 9.15 a.m. but owing to the state of the roads the Batteries were unable to man up to their and it was 12 noon before the column started. The route was via HARDIFORT, WEMAERS-CAPPEL, ZUYTPEENE, LES TROIS ROIS and LE NIEPPE to RENESCURE. H.Q. arrived at 4.30 p.m. I II & III were held up between ZUYTPEENE and LES TROIS ROIS by snow drifts and slippy surface in Hill & did not arrive in camp till 5 a.m. 4th inst.	
	4th		On arrival at RENESCURE No I Sec proceeded to ST OMER to entrain. They were there till 5 a.m. but did not arrive till 6.30 a.m.	

WAR DIARY
or
INTELLIGENCE SUMMARY — 14ᵗʰ D.A. Column R.F.A.

Army Form C. 2118.

(Erase heading not required.)

Instructions regarding War Diaries and Intelligence Summaries are contained in F.S. Regs., Part II. and the Staff Manual respectively. Title pages will be prepared in manuscript.

Place	Date	Hour	Summary of Events and Information	Remarks and references to Appendices
RENESCURE	Jany 4ᵗʰ 1915		Billeting parties were again sent on ahead by train from ST OMER. II & III Sections and H.Q.s rested to-day.	
	5ᵗʰ		The Column less Noˑ1 Section entrained at ST OMER for EDGEHILL. Thaw set in and roads melted and became less slippy.	
ETINEHEM	6ᵗʰ		After about an 8 hour journey the Column arrived at EDGEHILL & detrained. H.Q.s marched via MEHULTE and BRAY to ETINEHEM where Noˑ1 Section had already arrived. Noˑ II Section marched to LANEUVILLE and IIIʳᵈ Section to ECLUSIERES. The roads are icebound and bad for horse traffic.	
	7ᵗʰ 23		Rapid thaw set in today however and ice just disappearing. Billeting parties were sent off this morning to billet in the ROYE area.	
SEPT FOURS	2ᵗʰ		The Column has been on its march curtail today. During the day at ETINEHEM the CRA instructed the men of H.Q.s Noˑ1 and III Section Thaw proceeded even also adopted and in consequence about 20 teams were out daily hauling fuel and stores. The Column marched at 9.30 this morning and proceeded	

WAR DIARY
or
INTELLIGENCE SUMMARY.

(Erase heading not required.)

Army Form C. 2118.

14th D.A.C. 90 Y.A.

Place	Date 1916	Hour	Summary of Events and Information	Remarks and references to Appendices
SEPT FOURS	Jany 24		via FROISSY, ROSIERES, MEHARICOURT, FRANSART and LIANCOURT to SEPT FOURS arriving there at 4 pm. No 1 is situated at GRUNY. No II and III at ETALON and HERLY HQs is at SEPT FOURS	
GUISCARD	25		The Column marched from SEPT FOURS at 9.30 am this morning and proceeded to GUISCARD via ERCHEU and FRENICHES arriving at 3.30 pm. All Subord have been under cover but hours in out in the open. Peaceful weather has been experienced during the two days march. The 14th D.A. is taking over from the 154th French Division and part of the 62nd French Division.	
	26		The 1st M.T. Collative billet in DETROIT BLUE and DETROIT ANNOIS to enable to take up those in the former as French Henry Aibby are not moving out for some days	
CUGNY	30		No 1 Section overfired DETROIT ANNOIS and remainder overfired turnpikes billets in CUGNY and FLAVY-LE-MARTEL. Horses were put in open ends stables suspected for Mange.	

O.W.Birch Lt.Col.
Cmdt 14 D.T.C.

Army Form C. 2118.

WAR DIARY
or
INTELLIGENCE SUMMARY.   14TH D.A.C. — R.F.A.

(Erase heading not required.)

M 30

Place	Date	Hour	Summary of Events and Information	Remarks and references to Appendices
	FEB. 1918.			
CUGNY.	1.		2nd Lts W.J. COULTER and W.E. NEWLAND's Army joined My column are posted to II / S.A.A. section respectively.	
	3.		S.A.A. Section moved from FLAVY-LE-MARTEL with their permanent Artillery at DETROIT BLEU.	
			Lt. HORSBURGH 7TH K.R.R.C. is attached to I Sec. for duty. II Sec and H.Q. moved from CUGNY to permanent Artillery at DETROIT -	
DETROIT BLEU.	5.		BLEU. The Column is now situated as follows. I Sec DETROIT D'ANNOIS R.28 c 1.8. II / SAA Sec DETROIT BLEU R.34 to 6.6 and R.28 d R.34 to 6.8. H.Q. LA FERME ROUGE R.34 a 6.8. Shell 66 D. All Men placed have been turned out and distributed by the Hun. Accommodation for Officers & Men is in Armin huts and alone built by the French. The horses are out in the open without shelter and tied as for French & Belfort. Horses have been clipped and arrangement for preventive against mange.	
	6.		84819 Sgt. P. CUTHBERT S.A.A. Sec. awaited Croix de Guerre.	
	11.		C.R.A. 14TH D.A. visited the Column and inspected the camps at DETROIT BLEU and DETROIT ANNOIS.	

WAR DIARY
INTELLIGENCE SUMMARY. 14TH D.A.C. - R.F.A.

Army Form C. 2118.

Place	Date	Hour	Summary of Events and Information	Remarks and references to Appendices
DETROIT BLEV	FEB 1916			
	11.		Stables have been disinfected and whitewashed and all animals are now under cover.	
	13.		Lt. HORSBURGH (attached No 1) evacuated to Hospital.	
	14.		The few civilian inhabitants there are in the villages are without means to cultivate their land having no horses. The Column has undertaken the cultivation of adjoining fields and is getting ploughs into order and carting manure from dumps near the stables and spreading it on the fields.	
	16.		Capt. J. PENROS. S.A.A. Sec. proceeded a 14 days leave to U.K. 2/Lt. GRAY having joined the Column is attached to S.A.A. Sec. Lt. (A/Major) W.E. GRETTON having joined is attached to No. II Sec and assumed command thereof. Men are now 5 ploughs at work each working about 6 hours daily.	
	18.		2/Lt. W.E. NEWHADS S.A.A. Sec. proceeded to II Army T.M. School	
	19		for course of instruction. Capt. SWEENY M.R.C. U.S.A. regimental 44TH F.A. and class to be attached as M.O. 7/c 14TH DAC.	

Army Form C. 2118.

WAR DIARY
or
INTELLIGENCE SUMMARY. 14TH D.A.C. — R.F.A.
(Erase heading not required.)

Place	Date	Hour	Summary of Events and Information	Remarks and references to Appendices
DETROIT BLEU	FEB 1916			
	25.		Col. A.H.C. BIRCH. D.S.O. proceeded on 14 days leave to U.K. during his absence Maj. GRETTON assumes command.	
	26		Lt. STUART. TL Sec proceeded on 14 days leave to U.K.	
	27.		Capt. STEPHENS. R.A.M.C. rejoined from extended leave in U.K. Fine spring weather has been experienced and good progress has been made with all work in hand, e.g. Ploughing, Entire splints, harness, mud walls round stables & mud roofs. Cleaning up camp etc etc.	
	28.		Evacuations during month O. 2 O.R. 22 Animals 6.	

W.C. Taylor, Capt. & adj.
for O.C. 14TH D.A.C.

In The Field.
28/2/16.

14th Divisional Artillery

14th DIVISIONAL AMMUNITION COLUMN R.F.A.

MARCH 1918

Army Form C. 2118.

WAR DIARY
or
INTELLIGENCE SUMMARY. 14TH D.A.C. R.F.A. Vol 31

(Erase heading not required.)

Instructions regarding War Diaries and Intelligence Summaries are contained in F. S. Regs., Part II. and the Staff Manual respectively. Title pages will be prepared in manuscript.

Place	Date	Hour	Summary of Events and Information	Remarks and references to Appendices
DETROIT BLEU.	MARCH 1918 1		2/LT S. KILLE R.F.A. joined and is attached temporarily to II Sec 14TH D.A.C. from D/47 Bde R.F.A.	
	2-4		Snowy weather. Snow fell each day and all work in field was for time being stopped.	
	5		The adjutant attended a lecture on Economy in Government Material at Corps H.Q. For the first time since arrival at DETROIT BLEU ammunition was taken up to Battery position tonight.	
	7		Capt. J. PENROSE and LT. CROMPTON and 4 N.C.O.s left for ROUEN to attend a course in "Handling Indians". This unit is a view personnel in the DAC to the ultimate substitution of Natives for British sowing wheat	
	8		Having delayed I hammered the Enemy in started sowing wheat for the Armed Civilians today.	
	14		Capt. S.J. ALEXANDER and LT. M.McN HUGHES late of II Sec 14TH D/A. having been placed under arrest on 11/12 Jan 1918, tried by G.C.M. on 23 Jan 1918 had their cases promulgated today, the sentences being in the case of Capt ALEXANDER "Dismissed the Majesty's Service" in that of Lt HUGHES. "Severe Reprimand". A draft of 5 drivers R.F.A. arrived today. They were all posted to Brigades.	

WAR DIARY
or
INTELLIGENCE SUMMARY. 14TH D.A.C. — R.F.A.

Army Form C. 2118.

(Erase heading not required.)

Place	Date	Hour	Summary of Events and Information	Remarks and references to Appendices
DETROIT BLEU	MARCH 1918 15th		Capt. S.J. ALEXANDER left to proceed to the base under orders this morning.	
	16th		Lt. GRAY drew 44 remounts from HAM Rly.	
	17		7 day wag distributed as follows 46th Bde 33, 47th Bde 3, DAC. 8. A draft of 16 Drivers + 3 Gunners R.F.A. arrived - posted in further notice 16 Drivers 7th DAC. 3 Gnrs.	
	18		Bt. Hughes left to join 5th A.F.A. R.H.A. + is struck off the strength.	
	19		2/Lt W.J. COULTER proceeded on 3 days courses cadre at PERONNE. 2/Lt W.E. NEWLANDS See left to join V/XIX H.T.M.B. and is struck off the strength.	
			During the early hours of the morning 4 a.m. enemy commenced a temp bombardment was opened in the circle of ESSIGNY.	
	21	Ma.m	D.A.C. received orders to "Stand To" + pile up to establishment at Corps dump FAIRLOVEL.	
GUIVRY		12 noon	D.A.C. piled up & ready to move at a moment's notice.	
BEAUGIES		8 p.m.	Received phoned message from S.C.R.A. the retiring as GERMANS had broken the line & were advancing.	
		9 p.m.	III & VII Secs SHQ on the move, proceeded via CUGNY & VILLESEUVE to GUIVRY. Arrived at GUIVRY 12 midnight + found the village just 7 troops on move in to BEAUGIES and reported arrival to R.A.H.Q. at CLASTRES.	

Army Form C. 2118.

WAR DIARY
or
INTELLIGENCE SUMMARY. 14TH D.A.C. —— R.F.A.

(Erase heading not required.)

Place	Date	Hour	Summary of Events and Information	Remarks and references to Appendices
BEAUVOIS	MARCH 1918 22		Whilst at BEAUVOIS various stragglers reported - also officers & personnel of XXY 14 T.M. B'y who had arrived in retiring from ESSIGNY. These are now attached to 14TH D.A.C. and split up between I II & III secs. Communication is established between D.A.C. & R.H.H.Q. by means of mounted orderlies.	
		12 mn.	Received orders to move to GRISSOLES. Column on march by 1 p.m. & proceeded via QUESNY & ST MARTIN. Arrived at GRISSOLES 3 p.m.	
GRISSOLES			Supplied amm to 169 & 298 Bdes R.F.A. & various infantry Bdes.	
		4:30 p.m.	Received orders to move to BEAUVRAINS when column arrived at 7 p.m.	
BEAUVRAINS	23	2 a.m.	Received orders to move to PLESSIS CACHELEUX. Proceeded via NOYON - ROYE road & LAGNY. Was held up by troops in main road for some hours arrived at PLESSIS-CACHELEUX 4 a.m.	
PLESSIS CACHELEUX	24	7 p.m.	Supplied amm. to 169 & 298 & reported for A.R? at LASSIGNY. Arrived to move to LASSIGNY after many stoppages in road due to French & British troops retiring arrived at 9 p.m.	
LASSIGNY	25	9 a.m.	Went from LASSIGNY & proceeded via GURY MAREVIL LA MOTTE & MARCHY to MAREST SUR MATZ when arrived at 12 noon. The roads were again crowded & it was with difficulty the column managed to get along Ammn re supplied to 91st Bde R.F.A., 298 & 169 & one R.F.H. Battery.	
MAREST SUR MATZ	26		Arrived at MAREST. Ammn was resupplied to 91st Bde R.F.A. 298 & 169 & one R.F.H. Battery.	

Army Form C. 2118.

WAR DIARY
or
INTELLIGENCE SUMMARY. 14TH D.A.C — R.F.A.

(Erase heading not required.)

Place	Date	Hour	Summary of Events and Information	Remarks and references to Appendices
MAREST SUR MATZ	MARCH 1918 26		By 6 p.m. all ammunition and men returned to Column is now empty waiting to refit.	
	27.		Refilled with amm at MONCHY HUMIERES. issued to 36th, 18th, 20th & 14th DA also to O Bty R.H.A. 169 & 298 Bdes A.F.A. 4 Lt guns and 40 O.R. which had been attached to 169 Bde Lt were joined to D.A.C. and an extra sup party with them.	
		4 p.m.	Received orders for S.A.A. section to proceed to LACHELLE when they became attached to 14th Division. 169 Bde A.F.A. came in to refit and dumped all their amm in D.A.C.	
	28	1.30 p.m	Orders were received for No I Section to proceed to MOREUIL SUR MATZ with a full complement of amm. and dump in 36th D.A. Heavy shelling about this time attempted to camp about 6 p.m. and repelled.	
ARSY.	29	1.30 a.m	Received orders to meet at 5 a.m. to ARSY. in met by four clays march to LŒUILLY 10 miles S.W. of AMIENS. H.Q. I & II marched out at 8 a.m. in firing line and proceeded via COMPIEGNE & VENETTE to ARSY when column arrived by 2 p.m. No billets were procurable. Lt. STUART, 2/Lt BROWN and party from A.R.P. rejoined D.A.C. and clear Lt. detached.	
		9.30 p.m.	Received orders to move on 30th to AVRECHY.	

Army Form C. 2118.

WAR DIARY
or
INTELLIGENCE SUMMARY.

14TH D.A.C. —— R.F.A.

(Erase heading not required.)

Instructions regarding War Diaries and Intelligence Summaries are contained in F. S. Regs., Part II. and the Staff Manual respectively. Title pages will be prepared in manuscript.

Place	Date	Hour	Summary of Events and Information	Remarks and references to Appendices
NOROY	MARCH 30TH 1918	10 a.m.	Marched from ARSY via BAILLEUL LE SOC and ERQUINVILLERS to AVRECHY. Whilst en route Billeting party reported that D.A.C. was to billet at NOROY. Column arrived at 3 p.m. Weather very wet making marching difficult.	
		9.30 p.m.	Message received from B.M. R.A. reporting enemy aeroplanes believed to be in AMIENS-MONTDIDIER area. 2 mounted patrols consisting 1 Officer & 20 men were sent out to patrol N. of PRONLEROY and CREPON SACQ. These remained out all night and were recalled when column marched next day.	
ASSEVILLE ST. LUCIEN	31st	8 a.m.	Marched from NOROY via ST JUST and MONTREUIL to ASSEVILLE where arrived at 4.30 p.m. Weather good.	
			All animals and men extraordinarily fit considering amount of hardship experienced since 21st inst.	

In The Field
2/4/18

A.W.Walsh
Lt. Col.
Comdg 14TH D.A.C.

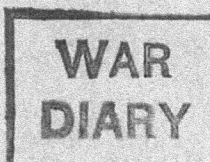

14th DIVISIONAL AMMUNITION COLUMN.

A P R I L

1 9 1 8

Army Form C. 2118.

WAR DIARY
or
INTELLIGENCE SUMMARY. 14TH D.A.C. R.F.A.

Vol 32

(Erase heading not required.)

Place	Date	Hour	Summary of Events and Information	Remarks and references to Appendices
SAUCHOY	APRIL 1/18	8 a.m.	HQ. I & II Sections marched and proceeded via MAVERS and FRANCASTE to SAUCHOY. HQ & II billeted at SAUCHOY. I Sec at DOMELIERS. Weather fine & own skinny - received orders for further march at 9.30 p.m.	
CONTRE	2	9 a.m.	Column marched & proceeded via LAVACQUERIE and BELLEUSE to CONTRE when arrived at 1 p.m. HQ. billeted in CHATEAU I & II in Jam. Entrails sent out to R.A.H.Q. 14 D.A. at POIX for ordnance stores urgently required. e.g. Horse Shoes, Nails which sent to CONTRE.	
	3		Today the column rested at CONTRE — began own workout of ground and harness cleaned and repaired. Received notice to move on to POIX to collect	
	4		Received notice to move on 5th inst. Lt Browne was sent up to POIX to collect stores. 14/15 amm wagons & 2 4.5 amm wagons taken by column to replace those received. No 298 A.F.A. also gave stores wheel poles oil & ghee.	
VERS	5	8 a.m.	Marched & proceeded independently to VERS when arrived at 12 noon. No 295 Bdy A.F.A. & No 91- Bdy R.F.A. arrivals in Jam, own motor cars. In truck & transport to BLANGY TRONVILLE 6th inst. A.F.A. Under orders to march to BLANGY TRONVILLE 6 Y.	
BLANGY TRONVILLE	6	10 a.m.	Marched 10 a.m. from VERS and proceeded via SALEUX and reaching B.Y. AMIENS and LONGNEAU towards BLANGY-TRONVILLE - being met by artillery party who had reported to S.C.R.A. 16 D.A. but who guided column into camp in open return BLANGY and GEISY. Received nearest 62 D. 1/40.000 HQ. I & II set in Jam at N 29 central. Reported arrival to S.C.R.A. 16 D.A. & 14 D.A. presently. Now under orders of 16 D.A.	

WAR DIARY
or
INTELLIGENCE SUMMARY.

Army Form C. 2118.

Place	Date	Hour	Summary of Events and Information	Remarks and references to Appendices
GLISY	April 1918 6		Got in touch with 16 D.A.C. from whom in due course and picked up & established Receipt value to get in touch with 46 & 47 Bdes R.F.A. for amm supply. 46 Bde Wagon lines at N 22 c. 47 Bde wagon lines at O 22. Batteries in action at O 21 & O 22.	
	7		16 D.A. moved out & came under orders of 5th Australian D.A. 58 D.A.C. moved into camp evacuated by 16 D.A.C. who had moved out. Arranged with 58 D.A.C. to form separate H.R.P.'s and divide amm army by lorries into two dumps. Lt-STUART put i/c 14 H.R.P. now established at N 21 c 4.1. Totham arch dump of amm from 277 H.F.A. at N 22 d 3.6. An learning that 46 & 47 Bdes R.F.A. were short of personnel & officers officers & n.c.o's then Bdes who had been attached to us since MAREST SUR MATZ were asked to rejoin their batteries forthwith. Stores e.g. shoes clothing etc. urgently needed were drawn from D.A.D.O.S. 14 Div at SALOUEL.	
SOMME	8		Amm Supply to batteries started. Returned on 8/4/7 lorries. Supplies of amm being drawn from III Corps Park in AMIENS. Weather very bad & transport lines in a bad state due to heavy rains. [illegible]	

Army Form C. 2118.

WAR DIARY
or
INTELLIGENCE SUMMARY. 14TH D.A.C. — R.F.A.
(Erase heading not required)

Place	Date	Hour	Summary of Events and Information	Remarks and references to Appendices
GUISY	APRIL 1918 9th		2/Lt. J.P. GRAY whilst out riding met with an accident & was admitted to a C.C.S. and evacuated.	
	11th		58th D.A.C. moved out this afternoon. The 58 A.R.P. at N26.C X Roads will also 12,000 Rounds was taken over by 14 DAC. The 14 A.R.P. at N21.C. was closed today whilst not met this no the dump at N36.C. is closed.	
	12th		Lt. PEPPER joined DAC from D/46 Bde R.F.A. and is posted to No.1 Section. 1, 6 and 3 inch Gun complete with horses and 1.18 pdr Q.F. amn. lorry rec'd today. Handed over to C/46 Bde R.F.A.	
	13th		About 20 wagons per day are out supplying amn. to Batteries of 14 & 47 Bdes.	
	16th		Received instructions to march on 17th inst.	
	17th		Lt. PEPPER and party sent to PICQUIGNY to collect 10 remounts. They are 6 horses & 4 mules in very poor condition. All amn. was dumped at 14 H.A.R.P. and dump handed over to 20TH D.A.C. who relieved 14 DAC. The 14 DAC marched out empty at 2 p.m. today and proceeded via LAMOTTE, CAMON, RIVERY, LONGPRÉ and DREUIL to AILLY SUR SOMME when arrived at 7 p.m.	
AILLY SUR SOMME.	18th		Rested all day at AILLY. Received verbal orders from B.M.R.H. & S.C.R.A. 14 D.A.C. to march to enthrone tomorrow 19th inst. The 14 D.A. on changing front & moving into 1st ARMY area near AIRE SUR LA LYS.	
	19th		H.Q. & No.1 Sec of 14 DAC marched at various times from 7 A.M. onwards	

Army Form C. 2118.

WAR DIARY
or
INTELLIGENCE SUMMARY. 14 D.A.C. R.F.A.
(Erase heading not required.)

Place	Date	Hour	Summary of Events and Information	Remarks and references to Appendices
	20th		to HANGEST SUR SOMME. when they entrained and proceeded to AIRE when they detrained in 20th & 21st. H.Q. entrained at 10.15 a.m. moved off at 1.15 & arrived at AIRE at 11 p.m. detrained and marched at 2 a.m. to WESTREHEM S.W. of THEROUANNE SUR LA LYS. when arrived at 5 a.m. No II Sec entrained at various times with Batteries of 47th Bde. and detrained at AIRE and proceeded to WESTREHEM also No I Sec 14 D.A.C. proceeded to SALEUX Sq AMIENS and entrained at various times with Batteries of 46th Bde. They detrained at BERGUETTE and marched to NIELLES LES THEROUANNE.	
WESTREHEM. 21st.			14 th D.A.C. is now located as follows. H.Q. & II Sec WESTREHEM I Sec NIELLES. LES PRESSES. S.A.A Sec and still attached to 14 Div	
	24th		The C.R.A 14 D.A. visited H.Q. I & II & inspected Mr Horses. Received orders to the effect that S.A.A. section 14 D.A.C. is to be disbanded - mules are to by sent to Army and animals and men dispersed as reinforcements	

WAR DIARY

INTELLIGENCE SUMMARY. 14 D.A.C. R.F.A.

Army Form C. 2118.

Place	Date	Hour	Summary of Events and Information	Remarks and references to Appendices
WESTRE-HEN	APRIL 1918. 22		Maj. Gen. VAUGHAN G.H.Q. inspected animals of I Sec. & H.Q. 2/Lt. Brown posted to 46th Bde. Capt. W.E. CRETTON to 47th Bde.	
	23		2/Lt. O. BRAND posted to No I Sec. 14 DAC from 46 Bde. S.A.A. section rejoined the 14 DAC and an additional at NIELLES. C.R.A. & B.M.R.A. visited S.A.A. and inspected horses. Orders received to fit up amm. from LAMBRES. Amm dumped by M/Tm. Lorries at WESTREHEN.	
	25		Yn S.A.A. Sec. was distributed today – new animals were disposed of as follows. R. L.D.H. L.D.M. Present 46 — 47 O.R. 46 12 18 47 5 36 47 — 22 O.R. I.S.I. DAT. 3 26 R.A. Reinforcement camp. 63 O.R.	
	26 27 28		Remainder of S.A.A. disposed of. 24 G.S. 13 L.G.S. wagons 1 water cart 1 Bicycle sent to Amm. Harness. Rifles stores sent to DADOS. Received orders to move 29th inst. New amm wagons of I Sec. handed over to D/46 in exchange for ribs without brakes. Bottoms all fitted 3rd DA of Amm. dump at WESTREHEN.	
LAPUGNOY	29.		14 DAC marched independently by Billeting parties left at 7 a.m. and DAC marched independently by sections at 9 a.m. to LAPUGNOY when arrived by 5 p.m. Billets were taken on for 50 DAC when in reserve – no amn was	

WAR DIARY or INTELLIGENCE SUMMARY.

14 D.A.C. — R.F.A.

(Erase heading not required.)

Army Form C. 2118.

Place	Date	Hour	Summary of Events and Information	Remarks and references to Appendices
LAPUGNOY	APRIL 30th 1916.		Lt BRAND and 22 O.R. tak over A.R.P. at D 11 c 4.5 a party was sent to 16 DAC at HAM-EN-ARTOIS to collect 53 L.D. Mules. Ammunition supply to Batteries begun. Amm is delivered to guns in action about V 18 & W 13 and W 26 27 & 28.	

In the field
1/5/16.

nnversmit
Lt. Col.
Commanding 14 D.A.C.

Army Form C. 2118.

WAR DIARY
or
INTELLIGENCE SUMMARY.
(Erase heading not required.)

14 A.T.C. R.F.A.
MAY

Not 32

Place	Date	Hour	Summary of Events and Information	Remarks and references to Appendices
LAPUGNOY	1		CAPTAIN J PENROSE and LIEUT. A. CROMPTON rejoined No 2 section from the Indian Cavalry Base Depot having finished the course in hardening Indians. LT G HOLMES is attached to HQ from No 2 section. The weather fine and dry.	
	2		Weather fine and warm. Sections did limes out on day fatigues for repairing roads. There were bombs dropped on LAPUGNOY railhead during the night.	
	3		The stonnards which were received from the 16 OTC were distributed. 46 Brigade received 12 L.D. mules. 47th Brigade 25 L.D. mules. No 1 section 14 Bdt 8 L.D. mules. No 2 section 8 L.D. mules. LA PUGNOY railhead 8 L.D. mules. HV shells about 6 were fired.	

Army Form C. 2118.

WAR DIARY
or
INTELLIGENCE SUMMARY.
(Erase heading not required.)

14. D.A.C. R.F.A.

Place	Date	Hour	Summary of Events and Information	Remarks and references to Appendices
LA PUGNOY	4		Weather fine but dull	
	6		The sections had wagons out on fatigues for road making also in wire meshes for ammunition to the batteries	
	8		Two Londm S.S. wagons and four other wagons returned from XIII Corps agricultural Supervising Officer SAVY.	
	10		The remaining two London S.S. wagons & the S.A.A section which were returned from the agricultural Officer SAVY. have dispatches & rations LILLERS for his mission to the base.	

Army Form C. 2118.

WAR DIARY
or
INTELLIGENCE SUMMARY.

(Erase heading not required.)

14 DAC R.F.A.

Place	Date	Hour	Summary of Events and Information	Remarks and references to Appendices
LA PUGNOY	12.		14 OR returned to no 1 and 2 sections from the 14 A.R.P.	
	14		There were a lot of items sent for ammunition for the batteries also F.C. beyond to move the 47" Bde wagon lines.	
	17.		BOIS DES DAMES and also the village of LAPUGNOY were shelled with HV guns during the day.	
	20		See Lieut- W J COULTER proceeds to the 47" brigade RFA 13 O.R. were posted to the 46" Bde and 10 OR to 47" Bde R.G.A. LAPUGNOY shelled at 10.30 am, 2 pm and 5 pm about 5 shells each time (calibre about 4.2 in)	

Army Form C. 2118.

WAR DIARY
or
INTELLIGENCE SUMMARY.

(Erase heading not required.)

14 D.A.C. R.F.A.

Place	Date	Hour	Summary of Events and Information	Remarks and references to Appendices
LAPUGNOY	21.		2Lt PUTTICK posted to No 1 Section from the 47 Bde RFA. Lieut J PEPPER attached to the 14" A.R.P.	
	24		One O.R. and water cart attached to XIII Corps Reinforcement Camp.	
	27.		LAPUGNOY Shelled all the day with guns of heavier calibre.	
	28.		LAPUGNOY again shelled during the day. Bombs dropped by 2 Lt KILLES of No 2 Section since attached to 47 Bde R.F.A.	
	29. 30.		Shelling during the morning and night of 29th 30th. Personnel Killed 1 wounded 8 Horses 8 Animals Killed 6 wire 5"	Quichbride Col

CONFIDENTIAL.

WAR DIARY.

OF

14TH DIVISIONAL AMMUNITION COLUMN, R.F.A.

From :- 1/6/18. To - 30/6/18.

Volume 38.

Army Form C. 2118.

WAR DIARY
or
INTELLIGENCE SUMMARY.
(Erase heading not required.)

14. D.A.C. R.F.A.

Place	Date	Hour	Summary of Events and Information	Remarks and references to Appendices
LAPUGNOY	JUNE 1915			
	1st		One officer, Lt LAMB, and 40 Other ranks employed in supplying French for Telephone wire	
	2,4,5, 6th		The whole was killed during these days	
	6th		Lt G HOLMES and 37 OR proceed to E THEROUANNE for 74 Remounts. 9 LD sent 15 HO 1 section 16 L.D. two 2 section and Remounts	
			(Lt G A BURNETT A.S.C. proceed to 15 Bde DAC) Lt Col BDL 20 LD and 10 R 45 Bde 16 LD and 5 Bde DAC 1.T. LAMB 13 and 20 Other ranks proceeded in lorry lorries	
	8th		No 1 Section handed over 8 LD mules to the 47 Bde RFA No 2 Section is moving to the 2nd DA and 3 motors from 3rd DA	
	9th		The shells of the wagon covered.	
	11th		The sections supplying & half limbers of ammunition R 330 RBE the sections supplying & half limbers of ammunition to the D.A.C	
	12th		Rev H OSBORN CF attached HQ DAC	
	14th		2/Lt S KILLE reposted to 2 section from the 47th Bde RFA where he was attached.	
			Section updates & information — H.Q. and no 1 section	
	16th		CAPTS TANNER attached the DAC on arrival from ENGLAND.	
	17th		The D.A.D.V.S. 3rd Div inspected the horses of the DAC	
	19th		CAPT S.E.L. TANNER joins the 47th Bde RFA	
	20th		Lt G CROMPTON attached the 14th ARP. CAPT PARKIN attached the DAC on arrival from ENGLAND.	
	25th			
	26th		LT. H. DAVIS to joins RFA DAC from the 47 Bde RFA.	

Army Form C. 2118.

WAR DIARY
or
INTELLIGENCE SUMMARY.

(Erase heading not required.)

14 DAC R.F.A.

Place	Date	Hour	Summary of Events and Information	Remarks and references to Appendices
LAPUGNOY	JUNE 1918 26		Lt C. STUART. of No 2 Section to Officers B.Po XVIII Corps Heavy Artillery	
	29		Lt. Holmes proceeded on leave to U.K.	
	30		The following Honors and rewards were subjoint during the month.	
			M.C. Capt. J. Penrose II/Sec.	
			M.M. Dr. H. Holdsworth II/Sec	
			M.S.M. A.V.C. Sgt. C. Maddams II/Sec	
			M.S.M. Farr. Sgt. A. Hood II/Sec	
			D.C.M. Dr. L. Parkin II/Sec.	
			The following are casualties for month.	
				Evacuated	Killed
			Wounded	14	1
			Personnel	2	—
			Animals	1	4	—
				CWCBirch Lt. Col.	
				Commanding 14 DAC	

Army Form C. 2118.

WAR DIARY
or
INTELLIGENCE SUMMARY. 14 D.A.C.
(Erase heading not required.)

Vol 35 R.F.A.

Place	Date	Hour	Summary of Events and Information	Remarks and references to Appendices
JULY 1918. LAPUGNOY	1st		Little ammunition is expended and consequently teams seldom take amn to gun line. Teams are 10 to 15 C.S. wagons are nightly leaving camp at 9 & army lorries at 3 & 4 a.m. They are engaged taking up R.E. material to infantry - also rations for rival regiments & ration ? "Pill Boxes"	
	3rd		Lt. S. WELSH proceeded on 14 days leave to U.K. A.D.V.S. XIII Corps & D.A.D.V.S. III Div. inspected all the animals. 7 hy arm wagons placed into Mun.	
	4th		All teams in amn wagons 2E, 48 are reduced to 4 Hy teams now. This leaves 96 animals. 7 Mm 24 cm to the transport spare in Vet Mun are now 72 L.D. Surplus 2/Lt KILLE and party proceeded to Base No. 4 Remount Depot with 41 L.D. hy road via THEROUANNE and DEVRES.	
	5th		Lt. O. E. BRAND proceeded on 14 days leave to U.K.	
	7th		The following surplus animals parted to Bases 4 L.D. to 46 Bde R.F.A.	
	11th		Capt. C. L. PARKIN R.F.A. left to join I Corps. 22 L.D. to 47 " "	
	13th		Lt. H. B. DAVIS II S/c posted to 47 Bde R.F.A. Capt. H.F. STEPHENS R.A.M.C. proceeded on 14 days contract leave.	
	21st		Ammn fatigue cancelled. D.A.C. engaged putting up splints - prov weeks at A.R.P. also carting slag for Inservation of new A.R.P.	

WAR DIARY
INTELLIGENCE SUMMARY

14 D.A.C. — R.7.A.

Army Form C. 2118.

Place	Date	Hour	Summary of Events and Information	Remarks and references to Appendices
JULY LAPUGNOY	1918 21st		Still carting up R.E. material - as Jr 17 & 13 Bde H.Q. I support tma. 7 enemy counties infantry in I Sec. 7 vans men engaged. 4 O.R. wounded. 3 animals killed. 12 wounded.	
	24th		Draft of 1 Off. 3 Sec. O.R. Jn 14 D.A. joined posted as follows 1 Off. 018 O.R. to 46 19 O.R. to 47 Bde. 10 O.R. to D.A.C. I Sec experienced further casualties whilst engaged on R.E. fatigue 1 killed 1 L.D. animals killed 3 L.D. animals wounded inj. 1 O.R. wounded	
	28th		46th Bde accompanied by I/14 TMT came under enemy fire 46 Div. No I Sec moved from LAPUGNOY to LES CHARTREUSES - D.24 d O.2. (BETHUNE continued sheet).	
	29		C.R.A. & B.M. R.A. 14 D.A. visited H.Q. I & II Secs & inspected arrivals.	
	31		D.A.D. V.S. III Div. inspected animals of H.Q. & I & II Sec. An enemy plane dropped bombs on I/14 TMT. Gun Park. Destroying 1 G.S. wagon & amm. Lt. Lamb killed 07 O.R. wounded. 17 47 Bde. A draft of 19 O.R. reported - posted as follows. 1 46 Bde. 1 D.A.C.	

Army Form C. 2118.

WAR DIARY
or
INTELLIGENCE SUMMARY. 14 D.A.C. — R.F.A.
(Erase heading not required.)

Instructions regarding War Diaries and Intelligence Summaries are contained in F. S. Regs., Part II. and the Staff Manual respectively. Title pages will be prepared in manuscript.

Place	Date	Hour	Summary of Events and Information	Remarks and references to Appendices

LAPUGNOY	July 1918 31st		Men getting casualties for the month.
			      Incurred Wounded
			 Personnel 10. O.R. 13. O.R.
			 Animals 9. 13.
			 Honours & awards. Military Medal
			
			 45896 Dr. J. Soulsby
			 58974 Gnr A.J.A. Cox
			 44588 Dr H. Anderson
			 81069 Saddler O'Carthy
			 99771 Sgt W.M. Mahathal
			 42376 Dr W. Ishan
			 93455 Dr R. Shanks
			 72737 Dr E. Kent
			 846205 Dr A.E. Holland
			
			      averench Lt. Col.
			      Commanding 14 D.A.C.
			
			 In the Field
			 1 — VIII — 18.	

Secret

D.A.S 2.9/8 109
2/ H.Q.
16 Division

Attached find War
Diary for July 1918, please

[signature]

O.C. No. 3 (S.A.A.) SECTION,
16th D.A.C.

Army Form C. 2118.

14 D Amm Col

WAR DIARY
or
INTELLIGENCE SUMMARY.
(Erase heading not required.)

Instructions regarding War Diaries and Intelligence Summaries are contained in F.S. Regs., Part II. and the Staff Manual respectively. Title pages will be prepared in manuscript.

Place	Date	Hour	Summary of Events and Information	Remarks and references to Appendices
	1918.			
Southampton	1-7-18	4 p.m.	Embarked per S/S. F.W. Miller (108.O.R.1.O.) S/S. Zariot (10.59.O.R.)	
Havre	2-7-18	8 am	Dis-embarked. Proceeded by road to Sarie (Blaville)	
Havre	3-7-18	15 am	Entrained.	
Denlington	4-7-18	8 am	Detrained.	
Hardinghen	4-7-18	10 p.m.	Arrived. 40 O.R. proceeded to 14 Div I.C. B's.	
"	5-7-18		Two officers + 38 O.R. arrived from Depot.	
"	10-7-18	10 a.m.	Left + proceeded by road to Bergues.	
Bergues	10-7-18	3 p.m.	Arrived Bergues.	
Bergues	11-7-18	10 am	Left + proceeded by road to Journalem.	
Journalem	11-7-18	3 pm	Arrived at Journalem.	
Journalem	12-7-18	9.30 am	Left + proceeded to Blue Maison	
Blue Maison	12-7-18	3.0 pm	Arrived. 1 N.C.O. + 4 men left for 14 D.T.M. B's. (1 chel.) 3 Horses annexed.	
"	14-7-18	5.0 pm	5 other arrived from 14 D.T.M. B's.	
"	22-7-18	10 am	Left + proceeded to	
Journalem	22-7-18	3.15 pm	Arrived. Interpreter arrived.	
"	24-7-18	8.0 am	Four G.S. wagons, 16 horses + 9 O.R. left for 14 D.N.Q's.	

Army Form C. 2118.

WAR DIARY
or
INTELLIGENCE SUMMARY.
(Erase heading not required.)

Instructions regarding War Diaries and Intelligence Summaries are contained in F. S. Regs., Part II. and the Staff Manual respectively. Title pages will be prepared in manuscript.

Place	Date	Hour	Summary of Events and Information	Remarks and references to Appendices
	1918.			
Boulogne	25-7-18		H/Mallinson C. B. 204984 struck off strength. Authy D.R.O.13 dt. 21/7/18 para 37.	
	30-7-18		Pte Botterley left for course at 26 M.V.S.	

ORIGINAL

Army Form C. 2118.

AUGUST 1918.

WAR DIARY
or
INTELLIGENCE SUMMARY. 14 D.A.C. — R.F.A.
(Erase heading not required.)

Instructions regarding War Diaries and Intelligence Summaries are contained in F. S. Regs., Part II. and the Staff Manual respectively. Title pages will be prepared in manuscript.

R.F.A. — VI 36

Place	Date	Hour	Summary of Events and Information	Remarks and references to Appendices
LAPUGNOY	August 1918			
	4		Lt. CROMPTON proceeded with 2 N.C.O's to attend a weeks gun course at XIII corps gun school.	
	6		The 3rd Div. was today relieved by 19th Div. and 14 D.A.C. came under orders of 19 D.A.	
	7		ENEMY shelled by long range guns.	
			2/Lt O.E. BRAND with 6 O.R. proceeded to join 1st Army school of Mortars for a course of instruction.	
			A.M. The day visited XIII corps amm. Representatives of H.Q. & III Section turned out to an fire gun along the BURBURE - LILLERS ROAD.	
	10			
	11		F/14 D.A.C. today received an 18 pdr gun from 46 Bde. This gun is for training purposes and a class of 1 Sgt. 1 Cpl. 2 Bdrs. & 6 gunners was immediately started.	
	13		Lt. G. CROMPTON proceeded to join F/14 M.T.M. Bty. and is struck off strength.	
	14		The yellow mine fired DAC gun Brass and am. Party to Section in place. I - 2/Lt. J.M. HUGO. II - Lt. R.B. LAMBE. 2/Lts. C.E. BENSON & F. FLETCHER.	
			2/Lt S. KIELE today proceeded to England is struck off the strength of H.Q. & III Sec. He was our only Sub. not	
	15		A.D.V.S. 19 Div inspected animals of H.Q. on condition.	
			Farriers are very busy getting their arm cut & brought in - in an keeping our men and animals.	

Army Form C. 2118.

WAR DIARY or INTELLIGENCE SUMMARY.

14 D.A.C. — R.F.A.

(Erase heading not required.)

Instructions regarding War Diaries and Intelligence Summaries are contained in F. S. Regs., Part II. and the Staff Manual respectively. Title pages will be prepared in manuscript.

Place	Date	Hour	Summary of Events and Information	Remarks and references to Appendices
LAPUGNOY	Aug 1918 17		Capt. Eastwood granted 10 days leave in France.	
	21		The following Officers having joined from base are posted to Sections as follows:— 2/Lts. R.W. MUSSON & McLEOD II; 2/Lt W.L. WILKINSON & J.C. STEPHENS I	
	25		1 motor cycle 2.E.D. horsen & 1 Dr R.F.A. arrived from base. Three OR taken on strength. H.Q. S attached to 59th Sec 14 D.A.C. The undermentioned officers are posted as follows:— 2/Lts HUGO & McLEOD 47 Bde, LT LAMBE & 2/LT. BENSON 46 Bde.	
	27.		The 2nd Gunnery Class started at M.I.S. section today.	
	28.		The following officers joined from base today and are attached to II/14 DAC:— 2/Lts T.R. LUNT & R.O.H. BOON. Also 12 O.R. from base.	
	29.		It has been on exceedingly hot month with frequent thunderstorms. Front has remained same. Rain was 1.80" in month.	
	31		Lt. C. STUART having undergone a month probation with Heavy artillery, is struck off the strength.	
			Casualties for month	Evacuated Sick
				Personnel armies 3 O.R. 2 Off nil

1/9/18.

[signature] R.C.M.
Cmdg 14 D.A.C.

20/

A.A. & Q.M.G.
14 Divn.

Enclosed, find
War Diary for August 1918.
please

[signature]
Capt R.3.A
O.C. No. 3 (S.A.A.) SECTION,
14th D.A.C.

August 1918

WAR DIARY
or
INTELLIGENCE SUMMARY.
(Erase heading not required.)

Army Form C. 2118.

Instructions regarding War Diaries and Intelligence Summaries are contained in F.S. Regs., Part II. and the Staff Manual respectively. Title pages will be prepared in manuscript.

Place	Date	Hour	Summary of Events and Information	Remarks and references to Appendices
Dunchin	1-8-18		Pte. Battonley left for course 26 M.V.S.	
do	4-8-18		96117 Jolliffe. Special Leave to U.K.	
do	4-8-18	7.10pm	S.E.1913 Nemn A.V.C arrived	
do	5-8-18	10am	14 Divisional Sports held	
do	7-8-18	10.15am	Two men left for later boat course at F.A	
do	12-8-18	5pm	Two men returned from 42 F A	
do	14-8-18	11am	Left & proceeded to	
Lumbres	14-8-18	5pm	Arrived	
do	15-8-18	-	Pte Battonley returned from 26 M.V.S	
do	16-8-18	9am	Left & proceeded to	
Dunchin	16-8-18	4pm	Arrived. Bdr Wyatt left for 26 M.V.S	
do	22-8-13	10am	Left & proceeded to Ledergem Area	
Ledergem	22-8-18	-	Left & proceeded to Wormhoudt	
Wormhoudt	26-8-18	-	Left & proceeded to Hannon Camp 27/F25 a-7-9	
Hannon Camp	28-8-18	-	Two horses loaned to R.D.M.O with two drivers (complete)	
do	29-8-18		Left & proceeded to 28/A25 b-0-8.	
28/A25 b-0-8	31-8-18		Bdr Wyatt returned from Stable course	

September 1918.

WAR DIARY
or
INTELLIGENCE SUMMARY. 14TH - D.A.C. - R.F.A.

Army Form C. 2118.

WO 95/37

Place	Date	Hour	Summary of Events and Information	Remarks and references to Appendices
LAPUGNOY	Sept. 1918 7th		II/14 D.A.C. marched to LA VALLEE 36A. V.10 d 6.8.	
			Left Group Commander there with us to solve + collect 18 pdr & 4.5" Hows amm from dot gun pits.	
	2nd		I/14 DAC. commenced salvage amm - salvage about 3000 rounds per day and dumping near Light Railway at BELLERIVE V.12 c.	
			H.Q. 14 D.A.C. moved from LAPUGNOY at 10 a.m. and arrived 11 a.m. offices + lines at- V.29 d 9.1.	
	5th		I/14 DAC. moved from LES CHARTREUSES near GOSNAY to BETHUNE 44 B. E.17 d 4.6. They are also engaged salving amm under M	
CHOQUES			Right Group. I/14 DAC. now under 19 D.A. 46 D.A. having moved out.	
	6th		Fine warm turn - heavy rain + thunderstorm - turns coming very hot.	
	7th		2/Lts R.O.H. BOON + T.R. LUNT posted to 47 Bde.	
	8th		2/Lt O.E. GRANT I/14 DAC. having proceeded to ENGLAND to join R.A.F. is struck off the strength.	
	10th		2/Lt J.C. STEPHENS II/14 DAC. posted to 47 Bde R.F.A.	

Army Form C. 2118.

WAR DIARY
or
INTELLIGENCE SUMMARY.   14 D.A.C. — R.7.A.
(Erase heading not required.)

Instructions regarding War Diaries and Intelligence Summaries are contained in F. S. Regs., Part II. and the Staff Manual respectively. Title pages will be prepared in manuscript.

Place	Date	Hour	Summary of Events and Information	Remarks and references to Appendices
	SEPT 1918			
CHOQUES	11		1 N.C.O. 20 O.R. reinforcements reported — all posted to Batteries	
	12		LT M.W. LAING & 2/LT R.T. DAVIES joined & posted to II/14 DAC. LT A.J.W. HORNBY joined & posted to I/14 DAC, and attached to HQ whilst performing the duties of 14 D.A. Gas Officer. 2/LT F. FLETCHER II/14 DAC struck off strength 12 — to ENGLAND.	
	13		II/14 DAC having completed exchange of ammn now LA VALLEE moved to HINGES. W15 a S.5.	
	15		Fine Weather again — general day	
	16		Received orders to move from VIII Corps area to STEENBECQUE area. C.O.C. R.A. & B.M.R.A. XIII Corps visited 14 DAC. H.Q. I, II/14 DAC marched from CHOQUES at 7.30 a.m. & proceeded via LILLERS - MOLLINGHEM & AIRE to STEEN BECQUE when arrived 1.30 p.m.	
STEENBECQUE	17			
	18		Marched at 8.45 p.m. in a clear night & proceeded via MORBECQUE, HAZEBROUCK & STEENVOORDE to an area ½ way between WATOU & STEENVOORDE when arrived 2 a.m. 19th	
STEENVOORDE	19			

WAR DIARY or INTELLIGENCE SUMMARY. 14 D.A.C. — R.7.A.

Army Form C. 2118.

Place	Date	Hour	Summary of Events and Information	Remarks and references to Appendices
STEENVOORDE	SEPT 1918 20		Locations as follows. H.Q. 29 K 15 d 4.6. I 29 K 15 d 9.1. II K 22 c 1.9. Lt. WILKINSON & 14 O.R. proceeded to ROBSON A.R.P. w.t 25.C 29 d 2.6 and took over from 34 D.A. a pack train of 90 animals and 4 G.S. wagons sent under Lt MUSSON to 25 C 29 d 3.3. to pack amn to A.B & C/46.	
	21.		Lt. DYKES granted 10 days leave in France. A working party of 150 O.R. sent to CORDOVA DUMP — OUDERDOM. S.A.A.S. & 14 D.A.C. located at 29 L 16 d 9.8 came under orders of 14 D.A.C. S.tumph: 4 Off 159 O.R. 19 Riden 168 L.D. 44 Vehicles	
	22		I/14 D.A.C. moved to new camp at L 23 d 8.5 (Sheet 29).	
	26		Lt. Col. A.H.C. BIRCH 'DSO, R.A., O.C. 14 D.A.C. granted 30 days leave to U.K. Capt. J. PENROSE M.C. R.7.A. commanding during his absence. S.A.A./14 D.A.C. now located at 29 L 16 d 9.8.	

Army Form C. 2118.

WAR DIARY
or
INTELLIGENCE SUMMARY. 14 D.A.C. — R.F.A.

(Erase heading not required.)

Place	Date	Hour	Summary of Events and Information	Remarks and references to Appendices
	SEPT 1918.			
RENINGHELST	28		H.Q. II/14 TMB moved from STEENVOORDE area at 8 pm 27th & marched to 28 G. 33 N arriving at 1 a.m. 28th. A fresh train 7 17 35 O.R & 35 animals has not to OUDERDOM to work under infantry division. Park Train returned.	
	29			
	30		Casualties for month. Evacuated 1 M 12 O.R. 2 L.T. animals	

In T.M 7 ill
1 - 10 - 18

W. C. Taylor. Capt + adj.
for Lt. Col. Cmdg 14 TMs.

Army Form C. 2118.

WAR DIARY
or
INTELLIGENCE SUMMARY. 14 D.A.C. - R.7.A.

(Erase heading not required.)

Vol 38

Instructions regarding War Diaries and Intelligence Summaries are contained in F.S. Regs., Part II. and the Staff Manual respectively. Title pages will be prepared in manuscript.

Place	Date	Hour	Summary of Events and Information	Remarks and references to Appendices
	OCT 1918			
RENINGHELST	1		Remounts (mules) arrived – posted to S.A.A. Section.	
NEUVE EGLISE	2.		H.Q. I II & S.A.A. Section moved to NEUVE EGLISE area at 8 a.m. and went into camp as follows. H.Q. 28 T 2 C 4.6. I 28 T 8 d 2.3 II 28 T 8 c 9.3 SAA 28 T 7 a 9.9.	
	3.		Started supply van to gun & Infantry.	
	6.		C.R.A. 14 D.A. visited sections and inspected animals.	
	8.		2/Lt C.V. PUTTICK regained from hospital.	
	9.		Lt MUSSON admitted to hosp as a result of a fall from his horse. Large amounts of amm 18 pdr & 4.5" How issued in readiness from guns – ordered & delivered to battery wagon lines.	
	10 11 12		Very busy taking up amm including A.B.B. for attack.	
	12		Capt Horn Division under II/14 DAC.	
	13		4 O.R.s & trans regained SAA from Current Party 14 Div.	
	14		2/Lt PUTTICK proceeded on 14 days leave to U.K.	
	17		Capt EASTWOOD on 14 days leave to U.K.	
GAPAARD	17.		Marched at 7.30 a.m. to GAPAARD AREA 28/0.35 – arrived 10.30 a.m.	

WAR DIARY
or
INTELLIGENCE SUMMARY. 14 D.A.C. R.F.A.

Army Form C. 2118.

Place	Date	Hour	Summary of Events and Information	Remarks and references to Appendices
	OCT. 1918			
KORENTJE	18		Marched at 8 a.m to KORENTJE - Nr COMMINES arrived 10 a.m. dumped 1496 A.S, 500 B.S. — 28/P 27 a	
LA VIGNETTE	19		Marched 7.30 a.m to LA VIGNETTE 28/W 19 central	
"	20		Rested at LA VIGNETTE.	
TOURCOING	21		Marched at 7.30 a.m to TOURCOING arrived 9.30 a.m — formed amm. dump at X 22 C.d.d. drew 3 guns 3 mirud to 4.6 Bde. — supplied 46 Bde with small amount of ammunition	
TOURCOING	23		CAPT J.S. STEWART proceeded to D.A.C. from ENGLAND. and was attached to No II section. 2/L MUSSON R.W. joined no 1 section from hospital	
	25		CAPT W.C. TAYLOR proceeded on 30 days leave to U.K.	
	26		A fatigue party from No 1 and 2 sections proceeded by lorry to ds dump at sheet 28 T7a b box and load ammunition	
	27		No 1 section supplied 46" Bde with a lot of ammunition	

Army Form C. 2118.

WAR DIARY
or
INTELLIGENCE SUMMARY.
(Erase heading not required.)

14 DAC R.F.A.

Place	Date	Hour	Summary of Events and Information	Remarks and references to Appendices
TOURCOING	Oct- 1918			
	29		2/Lt WILKINSON proceeded with 5 G.S. Wagons to old battery position at 28/D 36 b. Lt Col A.H.C. Buick returned from leave.	
	31.		Nos # 1 and II sections supplied to the divnal artillery for all the batteries of 4.6" and 4.7" How.	
			Casualties for month.	
			Evacuated 1 Officer Animals 3 & 26 H v S	
			8 O.R 2 destroyed	

AWCBurch
Lt-Col
Comdg 14 D.A.C.

Army Form C. 2118.

NOVEMBER 1918.

WAR DIARY
or
INTELLIGENCE SUMMARY.

14 D.A.C. R.F.A.

(Erase heading not required.)

Instructions regarding War Diaries and Intelligence Summaries are contained in F. S. Regs., Part II. and the Staff Manual respectively. Title pages will be prepared in manuscript.

Place	Date	Hour	Summary of Events and Information	Remarks and references to Appendices
TOURCOING	Nov. 1918. 1		A party of men in charge of Lt MUSSON proceeded to old ammunition dump at sheet 28/S 7a 9.7. to collect and load ammunition in lorries for new dump at MALCENSE. 29/T 25 6.5 10 G.S. wagons	
	3.		MARIE MUSCRON moved from TOURCOING to the following location starting at 10.30 hrs and arriving at 12.30 hrs. I sect 37/B 19 c 6.5. II sect 37/A 24 c 1.7.	
37/A 24 c 9.1.	4.		HQ 37/A 24 c 9.1. SAA sect - 37/A 24 c 6.9. All bvd 18 pr ammunition of No 1 and No 2 sections also 400 bvd 4.5" hvr sent to the 47 Bde R.F.A. 25 G.S wagons of bvd 18 pr ammunition sent by No 1 and No 2 sections to the 46th and 47 Bdes.	
	7.		5 G.S wagons in charge of Lt WILKINSON returned from CAPPARD where remnants returned to depot of munitions of 37/W & Th 33 Fr. TAYLOR Lt & Hon ME5 salving ammunition No 1 section moved to the purpose of sorting adjusting and salving	
	8.			
	10		ammunition of 96 Bde RFA and forming a dump of salved	

Army Form C. 2118.

WAR DIARY
or
INTELLIGENCE SUMMARY.
(Erase heading not required.)

14 D.A.C. R.F.A.

Place	Date	Hour	Summary of Events and Information	Remarks and references to Appendices
	11		M.G.R.A. 15" Corps inspected No 2 section.	
	13		C.R.A. Corps inspected H.Q. No 2 and No 3 (O.A.L) sections	
			Party working at HALCENSE dump returned to 40, and 2 section	
			9 L.G.S and 8 limbers returned from 41st 42nd 43rd Imp. Btries to the SAA Reft	
	14		8 limbers L.G.S. and 4 bodies L.G.S also 32 L.D and 16 O.R	
			attached to D.T.M.O. 14th Div.	
	18		20 horses reported to No 1 section dump to take away	
			bad ammunition	
	19-21		H.Q No II and SAA sections supplying limes & men I/c	
			ammunition for parties	
	22		No 1 section moved to ROUBAIX 37/A 20 d 7.2.	
	23		2 Teams attached to 14th D in Train	
	27		SAA section moved to 37/A 27 6.5.3.	
	29		6.G.S. wagons and limber attached to TOWN MAJOR TOURCOING	
	30		Ceremonial parade for the Corps Commander. No I and II sections	
			each turned out. 12 R.Q.F wagons with 4 horse teams.	
			Casualties in month. Officers Nil. Wounded 8 OR. Evacuated sick 4 L.D 1 R.Div	

CWCVBurch
Lieut-Col R.A.
Comdg 14 R.A.C.

Army Form C. 2118.

WAR DIARY
or
INTELLIGENCE SUMMARY.
(Erase heading not required.)

14 D.A.C. R.F.A.

Instructions regarding War Diaries and Intelligence Summaries are contained in F. S. Regs., Part II. and the Staff Manual respectively. Title pages will be prepared in manuscript.

Place	Date	Hour	Summary of Events and Information	Remarks and references to Appendices
	DEC 1918			
37A24691	2		16 Pairs of Wheels were sent to like captured GERMAN wagons from ROUBAIX station to Agreulline offices at AGNY	
			LES DUISANS near ARRAS.	
	3		No II sect moved to WATTERLOS. 37/A21 a.5.2. 20 GS wagons were sent to ROUBAIX before seals for lockkept tollos.	
	5		Six G.S. wagons daily for Town Myor WATTERLOS.	
	6		HQ 14 DAC moved to WATTERLOS 37/A 21 C 95.70	
37/A21C9570	8		All ammunition carried in G.S. wagons for gun communition and S.A.A. returned to COUCOU siding MENIN. 2 G.S. wagons became of the SAA section attached to Town Major MENIN	
	9		20 G.S. Wagons Sent- to TOURCOING to be used in sealing accommodation for a lockkept tallos.	
	11		Demolitions of coal mines commenced.	
	12		18 QF wagons - 12 18 Pr. and 6 4.5" How - Employed in collecting ammunition from railway siding dump at 37/C21a33 and delivering to COUCOU siding nr MENIN.	
	13		6t. CARPENTER arrived from the base with a party of 150 INDIANS which were distributed as follows.	
	14		HQ 14 I and II sects 31 SAA SAA sect - 74.	
			Lt Col D.M.H.C. Bird OSO proceeded on 14 days leave E.U.K.	

WAR DIARY or INTELLIGENCE SUMMARY.

14 D.A.C. R.F.A.

Army Form C. 2118.

Place	Date	Hour	Summary of Events and Information	Remarks and references to Appendices
ST ANICYTO	18		CAPT J.S. STEWART proceeded to LINSELLES with 38 L.D. horses and party of 24 O.R. in attachment to XV Corps Agricultural Officer. LT PRENTICE proceeded with draft of minor works to U.K. The C.R.A. and B.M. Major inspected the animals and lines of No 1 and No II sections.	
	19			
	23		CAPT J.S. STEWART proceeded to ENGLAND for duty at home authority. 14th D.A. Wire L.G. d/ 22.12.18.	
	24		Personnel and animals at LINSELLES returned to D.A.C. also Personnel and animals attached L-DTMD 14 DIV.	
	27		LT CARPENTER. proceeded on 14 days leave U.K. Teams and personnel returned to LINSELLES and DTMD upon return to DAC for Christmas.	
	30		LT COL A.H.C. BIRCH DSO returned from leave U.K. G.O.C. 14"Division" and G.R.A. 14 D.V. Artillery inspected No II section. 27/0 in 33 MENIN proceeded	
	31		Ammunition returns from railway siding dump. Casualties for month. Wounded. O.R. nil Horses 7 Bulus 4 L.D. 4 Mules	
			Demobilized Minor Practical men Walford Details 44 1	

A.V.C.Birch
Lieut/Col. R.A.
Comdg 14 D.A.C. R.F.A.

Army Form C. 2118.

WAR DIARY
or
INTELLIGENCE SUMMARY.
(Erase heading not required.)

14 D.A.C. R.F.A.

Vol 4

Place	Date 1919	Hour	Summary of Events and Information	Remarks and references to Appendices
37/A 21 c 95 70	JAN			
	1.		Fatigues were reduced by 7 teams.	
	3.		5 Brood mares were handed over to 26th M.V.S. 2Lt DAVIES, R.T. proceeded on leave to U.K.	
	4.		2 G.S. wagons were sent to ROUBAIX to assist 133rd French Div. arriving there.	
	5.		Lt WELCH returned from Hospital.	
	6.		Horses of Headquarters and No 1 Sect 14th DAC were examined by board and were put in Remount classes A.B.C. and D.	
	7.		Horses of No 2 and 3 (SAA) Sect were examined by board. Result 16 horses for Remount A 115 B 156 C 27 C-10 D 2	
	8.		Mules: A 190 B 88 C 49 C-1 D 1. No 1 Sect was examined by Remount board and were classified as X, Y, & Z. Horses of Headquarters and No 1 Sect were examined by Remount board and were classified as X, Y & Z. 6 Old pr, 12 men X, 10 men Y, 5 men YM and Bun Z Lt A.J.W. HORNBY assumed duties of ?/ADJT. Capt. and Adjt. HOLMES, G. proceeded on leave to UK	
	9.		Rev. A.H. OSBORN C.F. returned from Hospital.	
	11.		C.R.A. inspected animals of No 1 section	
	13.		C.R.A. inspected animals of No 2 section. 2Lt MUSSON proceeded with draft to UK	
	14.		Horse demobilisation camp formed at TOURCOING. 30 men sent there from DAC Teams and G.S. limbered wagons returned from French Mortars. Lt CARPENTER returned from leave.	
	15.		Capt. H.F. STEPHENS RAMC proceeded on leave to UK	
	16. 17.		B.Q.M.S. PAGE Hdqrs 14th DAC is awarded D.C.M. (auth. Wgazette of 4/1/19)	
	19.		Remount Board completed classification of DAC animals. Results for Horses X 151 Y 115 Z 42 for Mules X 183 Y nil Z 145	

Army Form C. 2118.

WAR DIARY
or
INTELLIGENCE SUMMARY.
(Erase heading not required.)

Instructions regarding War Diaries and Intelligence Summaries are contained in F.S. Regs., Part II. and the Staff Manual respectively. Title pages will be prepared in manuscript.

Place	Date JAN 1919	Hour	Summary of Events and Information	Remarks and references to Appendices
57 A 21c 95/70	20		Horses and Mules of Column were mustered preparatory to Demobilization	
	22		11 Horses (CZ) proceeded to LINSELLES for disposal	
	24		R.S.M. G.H.J. JAMES and L/BDR W. SOUTHERN were awarded the M.S.M. (Auth W.O. Gazette of 18/1/19)	
	25		CAPT. J.P.B. EASTWOOD and LIEUT. G. CARPENTER proceeded to ST ANDRE Concentration Camp for Demobilization. LT H.W.H. DYKE assumed command of N°1 Sect 14th DAC. A Sports meeting for Column was held.	
	26.		CAPT AND ADJT G. HOLMES returned to unit after Leave to UK.	
	27		16 Horses (CZ) were sent to LINSELLES 30 MULES (AZ) were sent to TOURCOING Camp for disposal. CAPT G. HOLMES sick	
	28		LIEUT R.H. Stanley WELCH proceeded to Demobilization Camp.	
	29		14th Div. Trench Mortars some broken up and Medium Battery personnel posted to 14th DAC	
	30			

CASUALTIES for month   Evacuated   Officers (Brit) OR   Horses   Mules   Indian OR
                                   nil   6   5   nil   4

Demobilized ——— Officers OR Horses Mules
                 3   197   32   30

CWCBirch
Lieut Col R.A.
Cmdg 14th DAC, RFA

D. D. & L., London, E.C.
(A5041) Wt. W1771/M2031 750,000 5/17 Sch. 52 Forms/C2106/14

WAR DIARY
or
INTELLIGENCE SUMMARY.
(Erase heading not required.)

Army Form C. 2118.

14 D.A.C. RFA

Place	Date Feb '19	Hour	Summary of Events and Information	Remarks and references to Appendices
In the Field	1.		44 AY Horses proceeded to Horse Collecting Camp TOURCOING for disposal.	
	2.		Lt. R W MUSSON returned from leave to UK	
	3.		all teams detached from the DAC were returned to section	
	5.		Lt. A J W HORNBY proceeded on leave to UK.	
	6.		3 animals of the column classified D evacuated to 26 M.V.S. Lt/Capt W M PRATT, Lt L A BRYANT and 2nd Lt C W STRINGER posted to the column from 4/14 and 3/14.	
	7.		C.R.A. 14 Div Inspected MTs 1, 2 and 9AA sections.	
	9.		Lt/Capt W M PRATT proceeded to St ANDRE Concentration Camp en route to ENGLAND for demobilization.	
	10.		7 AY and 13 Y proceeded to Horse Collecting Camp TOURCOING for disposal.	
	11.		CAPT H F STEPHENS R.A.M.C. returned from leave to UK.	
	12.		2nd Lt STRINGER returned from leave to UK.	
	16.		18 G.S. Wagons were sent by 1, 2 and 9AA sections to TOURCOING for carrying coal from railhead to units.	
	17.		18 G.S. Wagons again sent for coal fatigues.	
	18.		18 G.S. Wagons sent in support to DADOS 14 Div for conveying Indian native personnel from the columns from base. Lt. A J W HORNBY returned from leave to UK.	
	19.		3rd D.A.C animals sent to LINSELLES for 39 B2 and disposal	

WAR DIARY or INTELLIGENCE SUMMARY.

Army Form C. 2118.

14 DAC R.F.A.

Place	Date Feb 1919	Hour	Summary of Events and Information	Remarks and references to Appendices
NATTERLOS FRANCE	21		47 A* 69 B* and 6 C* were sent to the 46th 47th and 96th Bdes R.F.A. Lt. A J N HORNBY eft D.A.C. upon G.H.Q. scheme of chances (?) at LILLE.	
	24		19 AZ and 2 CZ horses were sent to Horse Breeding Camp	
	25		LINSELLES. 2 BY animals sent to Horse Breeding Camp TOURCOING. Vt-STRINGER to attached to 2 Army Field Remount Section PETIT RONCHIN.	
	26		15 AZ and 873 Z animals despatches to LINSELLES for dispersal	
	27		1 AZ riding horse despatched 15 LINSELLES for dispersal	
	28		54 BY animals sent to TOURCOING Horse Artillery Camp for dispersal. Cars were here for Month.	

Strength
Off   OR (Brit.)   OR (Indian)   Remounts
nil   9   18   1
Animals
Rt   OR
2   59   X · Y · Z · D · Remounts
Horses   122. 53. 133. 3
1 mule.

W. W. Wench Lieut Col R.A
Comdg 14 DAC

Army Form C. 2118.

WAR DIARY
or
INTELLIGENCE SUMMARY.
(Erase heading not required.)

/4 D.A.C. R.F.A.

Place	Date	Hour	Summary of Events and Information	Remarks and references to Appendices
ESTAIMBOURG BELGIUM	April '19 1		2 AX and 8 BX mules sent to LINSELLES have collecting camp. The Indian personnel of the 14 DAC left for FORGES LESTEAUX	
	2		to both & Z horse depots	
	3		6 AX, 7 BX riding horses and 2 BX mules sent to LINSELLES horse collecting camp. 4 mules sent for attachment to the 43rd Field Ambulance. 3 mules in team to 12th SUFFOLK Regiment were returned. The rifles and machine guns of the column were inspected by Lt SIMMONDS R.A.O.C.	
	8		Lt H.W.H. DYKE leave for 14 days to UK. 2Lt C.W. STRINGER struck off the strength & ambulance wk 15th C.R.O. 2DSt	
	12		3 Indian O.R. who returned from hospital were sent to 2 Horse Depot FORGES LES EAUX. CAPT. C.H.H. JENKYN and Lt. F.C. BLANCHARD 6th WILTS Regiment joined the column for duty.	
	15		CAPT. G.S.J. WOOD, 2Lt W.L. WILKINSON and 2Lt R.W. MUSSON left for R.A. Reinforcement camp COLOGNE on posting to Southern Divisional Artillery. Lt H.W.H. DYKE appointed acting captain (authority R.A.R.O. No 70 dated 18.4.19)	
	18		CAPT H.W.H. DYKE returned from leave to UK.	
	25		Lt Col A.H.O. BIRCH proceeded on 14 days leave to UK.	
	27		1 AX and 2 BX riding horses 14 x LD and 10 x LD horses 9 AX and 18 x mules were sent to TOUR COING horse collecting depot.	
	28			

Army Form C. 2118.

WAR DIARY
or
INTELLIGENCE SUMMARY.
(Erase heading not required.)

14 DAC. R.F.A.

Place	Date	Hour	Summary of Events and Information	Remarks and references to Appendices
ESTAIMBOURG	30		LT H W H DYKE left for R.A. Reinforcement camp COLOGNE on posting to services overseas artillery.	
			Casualties for month	
			Evacuated — Men nil OR 3 Indian Personnel 5	
			Demobilised — Officers nil OR Reposted 1	
			Sent to hosp & accepted — Men 4 OR 6	
			Animals killed/injury/escape — X. Y. Z. 40 — 1	

Signed
CAPT R.F.A.
T/Comdt 14 DAC.

Army Form C. 2118.

WAR DIARY
or
INTELLIGENCE SUMMARY
(Erase heading not required.)

/4 D.A.C. R.F.A.

Place	Date May 1919	Hour	Summary of Events and Information	Remarks and references to Appendices
ESTAIMBOURG	2		A party of men proceeded in lorry to BRUSSELS.	
	3		2 mules returned from 12 Suffolk Regiment	
	6		A party of men proceeded in lorry to BRUSSELS. All the Q.F. wagons, 5 G.S. wagons and water cart of No 2 section sent to wagon park at NECHIN station.	
	7		All the Q.F. wagons, 5 G.S. wagons and the water cart of No 1 section sent to wagon park at NECHIN station.	
	8		20 G.S. wagons, 11 L.G.S. and 4 L.G.S. limbers sent to NECHIN station.	
	12		One N.C.O. and 7 men sent to relieve MOUSCRON on guard duties	
	13		Lt. Col. A.H.C. BIRCH returned from leave to UK.	
	15		One N.C.O. and 5 men sent for treatment to 14 Div Canteen officer, 2 horses allotted to the column in lieu to OSTEND and YEBRUGE.	
	16		1 mule at Train lines 796 Bde R.F.A.	
	17		The Brigadier commanded or worked the column.	
	19		Lt.-F. BLANCHARD 6th Wilts Regiment having proceeded to Convent St ANDRE in route to WINCHESTER w repatriation ceases ble attached to the column	
	27		CAPT T PENROSE M.C. having proceeded to 2 horse depot ROUEN is struck off the strength of the column.	

WAR DIARY or INTELLIGENCE SUMMARY

Army Form C. 2118.

14 D.A.C. R.F.A.

Place	Date	Hour	Summary of Events and Information	Remarks and references to Appendices
STRASBOURG			Casualties for month Demobilised 1 O.R. wounded 3 O.R. Army H. RHINE 2 O.R. Repatriated 1 officer 6 " WHITE attached 1 mule 4 x 15 % 6 Bde RFA	

Winterbrook
Lieut Col RA
Comdg 14 D.A.C.

Army Form C. 2118.

WAR DIARY
or
INTELLIGENCE SUMMARY. 14 D.A.C. R.F.A.
(Erase heading not required.)

Place	Date June	Hour	Summary of Events and Information	Remarks and references to Appendices
ESTAIMBOURG	2		CAPT E.H.H. TENKYN 8 WILTS Regiment having proceed to for reperation excess kits attached to the Column 1/6 L.D mules proceed to the Column from the 91 Bde R.F.A. 210 mules returned from 10 H.L.I.	
	5		One N.C.O and 7 men returned from (pair) having at MOUSCRON. One N.C.O and 4 men left for transit guard duties at HALLUIN. One N.C.O and 8 men left for BISSEGHEM in pair duties	
	7		2 mules returned to the column from pack of the pannier mules 62 Fuel by R.E., 14th A & S.H and the MANCHESTERS. 2 L.D mules returned to column from cut of the following units 10th H.L.I, 42 Feld Ambulance, 43rd Feld Ambulance	
	11.		20 MIDDLESEX	
	12		62.65 wagons 3 water carts, and 1 Mother cart cruise car 4" vector, pick CROIX	
	13		1 N.C.O and 4 men returned to draft from drivers Base at HALLUIN. 36 18/pr Amm Wagons 12 4.5" How Amm wagons 11 L.G.S. complete and 4 limbers L.G.S. handed in to Vehicle Park at CROIX.	
	14.16.		1 NCO & 22 L.D mules sent to CROIX 1st Ethlin Cavy for himboard 76 O.R and 22 L.D mules returned from 13 Light North LANCS	
	15		Proceed St ANDRE for embarkation	
	18		~~Proceed~~ All stores and equipment of the Column handed to 6 Divisione and 1 G.S St CROIX 77 O.R to General St ANDRE for demobilization	

WAR DIARY
or
INTELLIGENCE SUMMARY.

14 DAC RFA.

Army Form C. 2118.

Place	Date	Hour	Summary of Events and Information	Remarks and references to Appendices
ESTAIMBOURG	18		Lt Col A.H.C. BIRCH, CAPT G HOLMES and LT L.A BRYANT left this column for demobilisation. 2 b.s having changed to vehicles park CROIX. 3 LD miles & TOURCOING have already camp. The 14th D.A.C. thus finds itself in existence - 9th and was peace.	1

AHCBirch
Lt Col RA
Comdg 14 D.A.C

www.ingramcontent.com/pod-product-compliance
Lightning Source LLC
Chambersburg PA
CBHW081407160426
43193CB00013B/2128